At the beginning of the 16th century the *Lomellina* foundered outside Villefranche-sur-Mer in the south of France. She was not discovered by a diver until 1979. It then took the French

Once cleared of sediment, the pieces of the ship's hull are marked one by one. It is the start of a long operation.

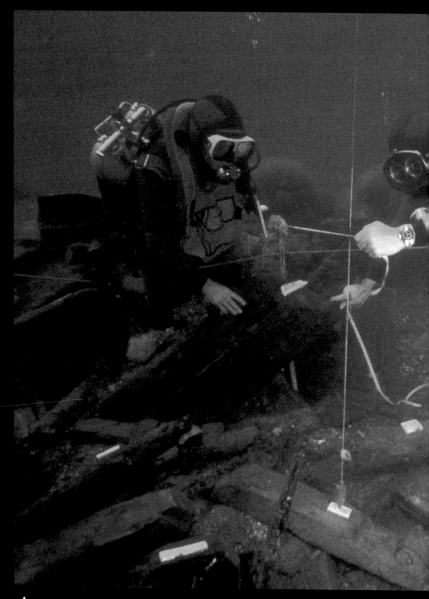

At a depth of 18 metres (nearly 60 feet) the archaeologists, visibly weightless, embark on the

A diver slides a camera along a metal frame. The photographs will help to draw up a plan of the wreck.

In order to study the basic shape it is necessary to perform an autopsy. Four-and-a-half centuries after the ship met its end, a diver cuts off a section with a chain saw.

After seven years of research the wreck is identified: it comes from Genoa, and is called the *Lomellina*.

CONTENTS

UNDERWATER ARCHAEOLOGY

EXPLORING THE WORLD
BENEATH THE SEA

Jean-Yves Blot

THAMES AND HUDSON

While land archaeology is a scientific discipline in its own right, its underwater counterpart remains a controversial area. A handful of professional marine archaeologists, ranks of amateurs, schools of divers and a fringe industry of wreck hunters all, for different reasons, lay claim to the unique heritage that humankind has left below the surface of the water.

CHAPTER 1

EARLY EXPLORATION

The diving suit (opposite) painted by Pedro de Ledesma in 1623 was imaginary; however, the pole was used by divers in real life to explore wrecks. Right: bottles recovered from the *Mary Rose* in a watercolour by the diver John Deane.

Breathing for the initiated

Through the ages water has been a virtually impenetrable blanket over the earth's surface. Until underwater robots came into common use in the 1980s, the central problem of investigating underwater remains related to the question of breathing: how could humans, bipeds without gills, survive, or even work, if only for a few minutes, in water? Half a century of using the aqualung

has done nothing to change the fact that water is an alien world. Half-fish, half-human, familiar with the unbreathable, the diver has always been someone different. He still is two thousand years after the *lex Rhodia* that regulated the recovery of sunken ships in antiquity, in terms of straightforward commercial salvage. According to a Byzantine version of the law, divers were entitled to keep a third of salvaged goods where the depth did not exceed 15 metres (50 feet) and half up to a depth of 27 metres (nearly 90 feet).

The Lake Nemi Renaissance

In 1446 the Italian architect and writer Leon Battista Alberti (1404–72) searched Lake Nemi near Rome, not for a merchant cargo but for traces of two great

Antiquities were retrieved from the sea even in days of old: a Roman stele (far left) found in Ostia near a temple dedicated to Hercules shows the salvage of a Greek statue that was caught in a fishing net in the early 1st century BC. The style of the statue suggests it is a bronze of the classical period, so it would have been four hundred years old when it was brought up from the sea.

Alexander the Great explores the sea floor inside a great glass cage in this 15th-century illustration (left). The legend originating in the first centuries after Christ presents the emperor-diver, exceptionally as a man who is content merely to observe.

On the order of Cardinal Prospero Colonna, a learned man in the Italian tradition of the period, Alberti (opposite below) brought divers from Genoa to excavate Lake Nemi. Demarchi (left) explored the Lake Nemi wrecks in a diving bell with a crystal side-window.

Roman vessels whose existence had long been part of local folklore, fuelled by the sporadic finds of fishermen. The lack of notable finds – mere pieces of wood from the wreck – did not deter the nobility of Rome from coming to inspect them. In Alberti's opinion the Lake Nemi wrecks dated from the era of the Emperor Trajan (52/3–117 AD). He was only slightly mistaken in his dates.

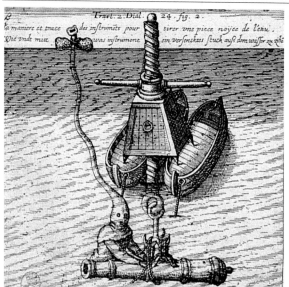

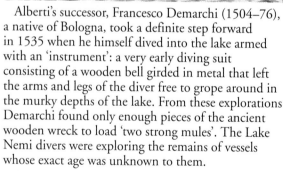

Alberti's successor, Francesco Demarchi (1504–76), a native of Bologna, took a definite step forward in 1535 when he himself dived into the lake armed with an 'instrument': a very early diving suit consisting of a wooden bell girded in metal that left the arms and legs of the diver free to grope around in the murky depths of the lake. From these explorations Demarchi found only enough pieces of the ancient wooden wreck to load 'two strong mules'. The Lake Nemi divers were exploring the remains of vessels whose exact age was unknown to them.

A heritage in cases

In the 18th century the discoveries made on land, first at Herculaneum, then at Pompeii, generated widespread interest in antiquities. Dedicated collectors such as William Hamilton (1730–1803), British envoy to the court of Naples, published their discoveries in magnificent works, which at times caused confusion: Greek vases were thought to be Etruscan.

The breathing tube-helmet illustrated in an early 17th-century engraving (above left) revived a fantasy drawn at an earlier date by Leonardo da Vinci that died with the discovery of the laws of barometric pressure. For two more centuries work under water was mainly undertaken by divers trained in holding their breath. They could not go any deeper than 20–30 metres (65–100 feet) and in most cases much less. On the whole they were searching for artillery, preferably made of bronze, and shipwrecks.

Initially a simple barrel, inverted and weighed down, the diving bell was perfected during the 17th century and soon came into common use. In 1664 divers in Sweden went down in a bell weighing over a tonne and raised bronze artillery from the *Vasa*, which had sunk 30 metres (100 feet) deep in 1628. A similar method was used in the Tiber. In the 17th century this river was so full of remains – some dating back to antiquity – that the Dutch engineer Cornelius Meyer made a plan to clear its bed, shown in his engraving (left).

In 1802 the British ambassador to Istanbul, Thomas Bruce, Earl of Elgin (1766–1841), ordered his secretary to have the most important friezes of the Parthenon copied and then taken to pieces. Some of the dismantled marbles were lost in a shipwreck south of the Peloponnese, at a depth of 20 metres (65 feet). Free divers (those who hold their breath while under water) from the island of Samos hired by

The frieze from the Parthenon below was part of the lot put in cases on Lord Elgin's instructions. The brig on which it was placed, the *Mentor*, sank outside Kythera shortly after departing for London.

the secretary took two years to rescue them. The collection was then taken to England and in 1816 Lord Elgin sold it to the British Museum. At a time when European intellectuals and artists saw Greece and her history as the crucible of western culture, the diplomat was later heavily criticized in his home country for the whole affair.

The Siebe diving suit

In 1819 the German inventor Augustus Siebe (1788–1872) was responsible for developing a simple and effective copper close diving helmet. The prototype was a miniaturized version of the diving bell that only covered the head. It was fed by a pump from the surface. However, this particular example proved to be too hazardous, as water flooded the helmet if the diver did not stand upright. In the final version (above) adopted by Siebe in 1839 the helmet was connected to a watertight suit, giving the diver great mobility on the sea floor; the apparatus was to remain unchanged for a century.

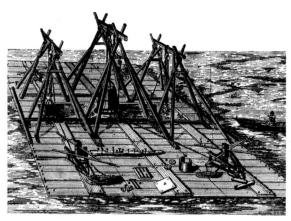

The two wrecks in Lake Nemi, a round, deep crater lake south of Rome, lay near the shore at depths of under 23 metres (75 feet). Like Alberti before him, the engineer Fusconi failed, despite his diving platform (left), in his attempt to raise one of the great wooden giants of which people had been speaking for centuries, though no one, apart from divers, had seen them yet.

In 1895 Eliseo Borghi, a dealer in antiquities from Rome, reinstigated diving at Lake Nemi. Sumptuous bronze lion and wolf heads were retrieved from the lake and also mosaics and stones (left).

Below: the 'Piombino Apollo', a 5th-century BC bronze made by the lost wax process.

The diving suit was still far from universally accepted in 1827 when Annesio Fusconi installed on Lake Nemi a large raft supporting a diving bell eight hands (2.5 metres or 8 feet) in internal diameter, equipped with an air pump. From the Roman wrecks, then dated to the era of the Emperor Tiberius (42 BC–AD 37), were retrieved a few pieces, some of which – marbles and mosaics – confirmed that these were no ordinary ships. In 1832 a statue 1.15 metres (nearly 4 feet) high, one of the rare archaic Greek bronzes known, was recovered off the Italian coast. Two years later France paid 16,000 old francs for the 'Piombino Apollo', now in the Louvre.

The Deane brothers and the *Mary Rose*

The divers John and Charles Deane, who started as
plain technicians, were in part to open the way for
historical investigations of underwater sites. Salvage
divers contracted to the British government, the
Deanes invented a rudimentary diving suit similar to
Siebe's prototype. One day in June 1836, when they
were diving over a wreck off the British naval base at
Spithead, fishermen asked them to investigate an
obstruction on which their nets often snagged.
John Deane dived at the designated spot
and soon saw the remains of an
old ship just protruding from
the muddy bottom as well
as a bronze cannon, which
was raised to the surface.
A committee of artillery experts
at the Tower of London,
who had been advised of
the find, recommended

Thanks to his
watercolours
showing artefacts
recovered by him from
various wrecks, the
testimony of John
Deane is unique.

that the divers continue their work. In the opinion of these experts the wreck was possibly that of the *Mary Rose*, a British ship of historical significance that had capsized off Portsmouth in 1545 during an engagement with a French war fleet. The identification of

the wreck had financial implications for the Deanes: if it could be proved to be a merchant vessel, they were entitled to keep their finds. They lost their rights if the ship were royal. The Deanes proceeded to raise from the wreck several pieces of artillery, including some that caused much comment, the iron guns, not 'cast' but 'built up' of wrought-iron staves bound by hoops. Up to this point it had been thought that such antiquated pieces of artillery were no longer in use at the time of the *Mary Rose*. As crown property, the guns reverted to the gentlemen in the Tower of London. However, the divers were entitled to lesser objects, which they sold at auction in 1840; among them were 'common glass bottles' at fifteen shillings apiece and eight 'warrior's bows'.

While diving near the *Royal George* (opposite), which sank at Spithead in 1782, John Deane found the much older *Mary Rose* (depicted in the period miniature on the left), which had capsized in front of King Henry VIII during a naval engagement in 1545. Apart from bronze artillery, the wreck contained wrought-iron guns (such as the one below) of an early date that surprised historians in 1840. At the end of the operations the Deanes were authorized to use explosives in order to probe the wreck.

Deane intended his watercolours for a work, which was never published, entitled *John Deane's Cabinet of Submarine Recoveries, Relics and Antiquities.* The many oak pieces of the *Mary Rose* were sold with other finds in 1840 and later made into a variety of objects stating the source from which they had come. The misleading impression was given that the hull had disappeared – until it was rediscovered in 1967 by a team led by the historian and diver Alexander McKee.

Fishing for bronze and iron

In the mid-19th century numerous underwater discoveries gave a new direction to archaeological research. The nations of Europe were searching for their roots and turned to their local undocumented prehistory, which comprised stone and metal objects. From 1836 the work of the Dane Christian J. Thomsen, curator of the Museum of Northern Antiquities (later the National Museum) in Copenhagen, made it possible to divide the evolution of the man-made object into three ages, progressing from the use of stone to bronze and then iron. The lakes of Europe would soon make a huge contribution to this new line of inquiry.

This 19th-century watercolour is typical of its time in drawing inspiration for lake dwellings on piles from the villages of Africa and Asia.

It all began with the prolonged drought of 1853–4, which lowered the level of the Swiss lakes and exposed rows of wooden posts to the open air. Ferdinand Keller, president of the Antiquarian Association of Zurich, who revealed the discoveries at Obermeilen on Lake Zurich, advanced

The bed of the river Thiele near the village of La Tène yielded over 2500 artefacts, including 166 iron swords (opposite) that bore witness to developed metalwork skills.

the idea that these forests of wooden poles on the lake shores were the remains of old dwellings built over water.

The 'fishing for antiquities' quickly spread to other lakes. In 1854 the Swiss Alphonse Morlot, equipped with a bucket fitted with a glass 'window', went down into the water at Morges on Lake Geneva and gathered objects between the wooden stakes of a Bronze Age lake settlement with a net. In 1856 archaeologists in France reported the discovery of the Grésine lake dwellings in Lake Bourget. Other finds followed in Lake Annecy and Lake Chalain. At La Tène on Lake Neuchâtel Colonel Friedrich Schwab, an archaeologist from Bienne, used

A collector of antiquities and occasional diver, Morlot is sometimes said to have pioneered archaeological research by diving. In the drawing above he shows himself at work. When he explored the lake dwellings at Morges in a diving suit in 1854 the site typically looked like a submerged forest of stakes. In 1875 the French prehistorian Gabriel de Mortillet coined the term 'Morgian' to refer to the earliest stage of the Bronze Age.

a dragnet to raise wrought-iron swords in 1857. These were not the usual lake dwellings. From 1868 hydraulic works on the Jura rivers caused the water level to drop 2 metres (6½ feet) and in 1874 the Swiss teacher Emile Vouga embarked on a thorough excavation of the banks. More than one hundred iron swords were found over an area of under 4000 square metres (43,000 square feet) but the customary evidence of lake-side habitation was absent: there were no accumulations of charcoal or kitchen refuse nor any other traces of domestic life. This launched a long debate on the precise nature of the remains found. Spanning five centuries up to the last decades before Christ, the La Tène site then became an established point of reference for the second Iron Age. More than twenty lake settlements were later to be identified in Lake Neuchâtel alone.

Over 1200 artefacts, most of them bronze, from the prehistoric dwellings of Lake Bourget were documented in 1875: socketed and flanged axes, sickles, hooks, daggers, swords, pins, bracelets, and also sandstone and mica schist moulds. Pieces of basketwork and carpentry, seeds and fruits were also found at Lake Bourget, as in Switzerland. The fresh water and fine mud had preserved these fragile traces of daily life. Fifty years later the French archaeologist Joseph Déchelette noted that 'these sensational discoveries were for a long time the archaeologist's main source of information on Bronze Age industry'. In fact, the finds from the lake floor related to a very long period. Archaeologists discovered more elaborate workmanship, associated with the use of metal tools, in the late constructions. From the end of the 1860s objects found at Lake Paladru in Isère, France, were attributed to the Early Middle Ages.

All these investigations were conducted on fresh-water sites. Archaeology in a water environment had been born, far away from the sea.

Visitors to the Universal Exhibition in Paris in 1867 saw a range of fine objects found in the Saône river, several of them from the Bronze Age. There was also a silver-plated bronze bust that was later identified as the 4th-century Roman Emperor Magnentius (below).

This 19th-century painting shows the La Tène site after hydraulic works took place in the Jura from 1868 to 1881. Among the various functions of the site suggested were a refuge, a military post, a sacrificial shrine, a regional or remote trading station; tin, glass, bronze and gold artefacts (left) were found there. Different reasons for the site's abandonment in the 2nd–1st century BC were also put forward: battle, fire, sudden or gradual flooding. Recent geological analysis has confirmed the theory of progressive inundation.

A late offshoot of the history of art, archaeology under the sea was born unexpectedly at the beginning of the 20th century. The human instruments of discovery, the helmet divers, carried out the first excavations alone on the sea bed. At first they were only expected to hunt for fine objects.

CHAPTER 2

WALKING ON THE SEA FLOOR

With the advent of modern helmet diving gear the diver became a manual and demolition worker, mason and salvager. A diver (opposite) explores the wreck of the battleship *Magenta*, which caught fire in the port of Toulon in 1875 while carrying antiquities from Tunisia. Rescued at the time was the decapitated statue of Sabina, wife of the Emperor Hadrian (AD 117–38). The head (right) was not found in the mud until 1995.

A treasure in Spain

One of the first to carry out a proper investigation of an underwater archaeological site was a French banker living in Spain, Hippolyte Magen. 'A considerable enterprise' had been proposed to him one day in March 1868. It proved to be a treasure hunt inspired by a rumour going back 150 years: a search for the riches of Spanish galleons sunk by an Anglo-Dutch fleet, which had just returned from America in 1702. It was said to be lying at the bottom of the Ría de Vigo in Galicia. Magen asked for time to think, made inquiries, and plunged into the venture – unaware that the greater part of the valuable cargo had been unloaded a few days before the battle.

Meanwhile, the French writer Jules Verne published *Twenty Thousand Leagues under the Sea* (1870), in instalments, detailing the story of the fleet lost at Vigo. Verne wrote of treasure that financed the dives of Captain Nemo, commander of the submarine *Nautilus*.

In his organized way, Magen put together the best diving equipment available in France and a team of seasoned divers. An engineer from Angers, Ernest Bazin, who had invented an underwater light projector, was recruited after the start of work. He observed the divers working in the murky waters of the Ría de Vigo through the side-window, 12 cm (nearly 5 inches) thick, of a diving 'turret', which in fact proved to be inadequate for the task. What was needed, Magen and his technicians argued to the members of the concessionary company, was a diver-inspector, better still an underwater master of works, to supervise the divers.

An adviser on Magen's team, shown at work on the Vigo galleons in the period illustrations opposite and below, reported that the submerged structures had disappeared under 'the devouring action of shipworm'. Several centuries of carving up the Vigo wrecks left nothing or almost nothing other than a few drawings and photographs: below is a piece from the

wooden structure of the so-called *Almirante*, raised by the Italian company Impresa Demolizioni Ricuperi Affuri Subaquei during 1928 and 1929.

Bazin reported strange chemical reactions in the decomposed objects that the divers raised from the muddy water of the Ría. 'Strangely,' related Magen describing an iron cannon, 'the cascabel is so decomposed that it gives under a knife like putty, whereas the chase is solid and rings under the hammer.'

The experiences at Vigo unwittingly pointed a finger at what were to prove the problems of excavating underwater sites.

One of the wrecks examined was the *Tambor*, which formed a bulge 1.5 metres (5 feet) high on the floor of the Ría. Having vigorously attacked it with torpedoes, Magen described the shell: 'It heels over to port, its port-side ribs emerge from the sludge and reveal a poorly buried part of the frame; those on the starboard side are totally sunk in the muddy bottom.'

All the artefacts were catalogued and put in glass cases in a special store. Magen only found in the galleons a little money, sailors' trinkets, tonnes of iron from cannons and anchors, and exotic wood, which was put on sale. The entire collection was broken up.

Killer conditions

A modern marine excavation project can involve thousands of hours under water. The first underwater campaign undertaken by Magen in Vigo in 1870 lasted five months, during which 744 hours of diving were recorded; on land this would have equated to ten days' work for ten men. In the course of their diving the men suffered from several unexplained illnesses. It was a few years later, in 1878, that Paul Bert, a professor at the Sorbonne in Paris, published his research on barometric pressure and put forward the theory that divers' illnesses were caused by diluted gas in the blood while they were breathing under pressure.

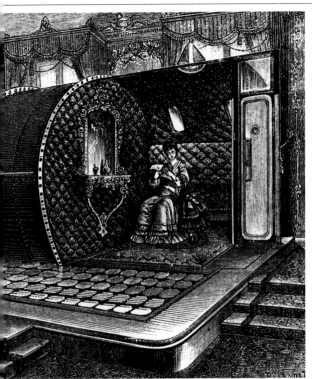

By supplying the diver with air at the same pressure as the surrounding water, helmet diving gear gave the false impression that water had ceased to be an obstacle. Subsequent accidents showed that periods in a compressed atmosphere are governed by very strict rules. A gradual, well-paced return to the surface is essential to ensure the safety of the diver and decompression chambers are used in the process. Paul Bert's groundbreaking study of the subject, *La Pression barométrique*, was published in 1878. A two-chamber cylinder (left) and the pneumatic chamber (below) are the basic tools of the early experiments.

In the spring of 1900 a group of Greek sponge divers returning from the African coast was forced, because of bad weather, to seek refuge among the cliffs at Antikythera, a small island north of Crete. One of the divers, Elias Stradiatis, made a routine dive at the foot of a cliff and discovered bronze and marble statues lying tens of metres deep. His boss, Kondos, who dived just after him, brought up a green metal arm. Soon informed of the find, the Greek authorities despatched a warship to the site in November of that year to support the divers, who this time were paid by

The Rouquayrol-Denayrouze diving apparatus (opposite) was chosen by Magen for work at Vigo in 1870. At the time it was already in use by sponge divers in the Aegean.

the government. Like the guns of the *Mary Rose* before them, these statues seemed worth any sacrifice. The Greek state was then only seventy-one years old as an independent nation and its ancient heritage helped to give it a sense of national identity.

Because of the depth of the site at Antikythera – between 40 and 55 metres (130 and 180 feet) – the men were only allowed to dive twice a day, for five minutes at a time. Over a period of nine consecutive months one met his death and two others were left invalids for life – the price of one of the finest collections of Greek art from the 4th century BC.

A few years after the casualties at Antikythera the Scottish physiologist John Scott Haldane conducted experiments with divers of the Royal Navy. In 1906 he published the first diving tables that were aimed at avoiding decompression sickness, covering depths up to 60 metres (about 200 feet). Deep enough, but too late for the divers at Antikythera.

Export ban on Greek antiquities

The finds at Antikythera were to cause disagreement between two Greek archaeologists: one was convinced that the well-laden wreck dated from the 4th century BC, like the bronze statues it contained; the other, after studying the ordinary pottery found by divers near the statues, judged his colleague was too early by three centuries.

The second theory, although based like the first on its author's personal intuition, proved to be right: fifty years later an archaeologist from the University of Pennsylvania, Roger Edwards, re-examined the material brought up in 1900 and 1901 and pronounced that the pottery from the Antikythera wreck came from the coast of central Turkey on the Aegean Sea. In fact, the bronze statues were already antiquities when they sank. As for the marbles, they are now known to have been copies. In 1965 the American archaeologist Virginia Grace examined the

The table of amphora forms (opposite) published by the 19th-century German scholar Heinrich Dressel provided the key tool for dating the cargos of antiquity: the amphora was a simple container contemporaneous with the vessel that carried it. Dating a wreck carrying works of art was another matter in 1900: these could already have been hundreds of years old on their final voyage. At the Antikythera site, for example, lay a 3rd-century BC statue of a 'philosopher' (above) and an 'ephebe' or young man dating from 340 BC (far right).

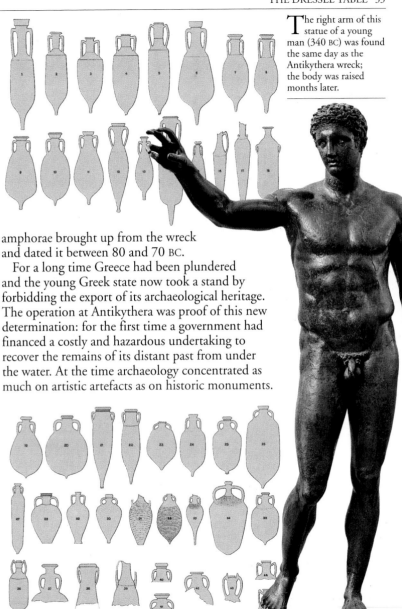

The right arm of this statue of a young man (340 BC) was found the same day as the Antikythera wreck; the body was raised months later.

amphorae brought up from the wreck and dated it between 80 and 70 BC.

For a long time Greece had been plundered and the young Greek state now took a stand by forbidding the export of its archaeological heritage. The operation at Antikythera was proof of this new determination: for the first time a government had financed a costly and hazardous undertaking to recover the remains of its distant past from under the water. At the time archaeology concentrated as much on artistic artefacts as on historic monuments.

Diving in the Chichén Itzá *cenote* (left) meant going down 27 metres (nearly 90 feet) to probe a thick layer of mud holding Maya artefacts, such as the gold statuette of a monkey below, thrown there as part of a ritual a thousand years earlier. Although Thompson bought the land around the *cenote*, the Mexican government later asked the Peabody Museum of Harvard to return some of his finds.

From 1904 to 1909 Edward H. Thompson explored an ancient sacred spring at Chichén Itzá in Mexico

Lost in the forest of the Yucatán peninsula, the remains of the Maya civilization had been studied on various expeditions in the latter half of the 19th century, the first going back even further to the Spanish monarchy in the late 18th century. In the 20th century Thompson, who was a United States consul, supported by the Peabody Museum of Harvard University (founded in October 1866) and by the American Antiquarian Society, had bought the plantation where the *cenote* (natural spring) that was to be explored was situated. He learned to use helmet diving gear and retrieved thousands of objects intact by using a dredging bucket. Two Greek sponge divers, part of a small community based in south Florida at the time, took part in the excavation.

Among the artefacts brought up in the 1340 hours of diving at Mahdia was a bronze herm of the 2nd century BC (opposite) by Boëthus of Chalcedon.

The consul-diver's simple 'harvest', gathered by groping in the muddy darkness of the *cenote*, came at the end of a period in which American archaeologists, as noted by Gordon Willey and Jeremy Sabloff in *A History of American Archaeology* (1974), 'struggled to make archaeology into a systematic, scientific discipline. They did not succeed; but they laid the foundations'. This was also true outside America.

Mahdia and its bronzes

In 1907 it was once again a Greek sponge diver who located an ancient wreck containing works of art, including marble pillars, 39 metres (128 feet) deep near Mahdia in Tunisia. Ancient Greek bronzes began to appear on the market, attracting the attention of Alfred Merlin, the head of the Tunisian antiquities department, who mounted a diving operation with the backing of an American millionaire living in Paris, James Hazen Hyde.

At the end of five salvage operations conducted from 1908 to 1911 and in 1913 by mainly Greek divers (and one Turkish), artefacts found in the sand, often still intact, filled five galleries in the Bardo Museum in Tunis. According to the French archaeologist Salomon Reinach, who wrote a monumental general history of the plastic arts, *Apollo* (1904), in which he predicted great discoveries under the sea, Mahdia had no equivalent outside Pompeii and Herculaneum, both of which had been explored since the 18th century.

Throughout the operations archaeologists and art historians remained on the surface. The Mahdia wreck dated from the 1st century BC, like the one found at Antikythera. Some sixty capitals, plinths and Ionic columns were left at the bottom of the sea because of the difficulties involved in raising such heavy pieces. Another fifty years would pass before divers and archaeologists returned to the site to look for something other than works of art.

Ranging from the aeroplane to underwater photography, the tools of the first half of the 20th century prepared the ground for the flowering, still some time ahead, of underwater archaeology. The real breakthrough came with the invention of the aqualung in 1943, which opened the door at last to a world that had previously been the preserve of just a handful of specialist divers.

CHAPTER 3

WHERE ARE THE ARCHAEOLOGISTS?

The Le Prieur aqualung, exhibited in Paris in 1934 (opposite), was a very early model requiring constant manual adjustment. The final version, which supplied air automatically, left the diver's hands free, allowing him or her to move around easily – even between the fragile posts of the Lake Neuchâtel dwellings (right) – without disturbing the seabed.

The Duce's pumps

The Italian dictator Benito Mussolini shared with the Roman emperors a taste for theatrical enactments of history, which he drew on for a propaganda campaign. The emperors of the 1st century AD had on several occasions staged great aquatic spectacles in which vast artificial ponds were filled and emptied to persuade the public of the supernatural powers of the supreme head of state. Mussolini confined himself to draining Lake Nemi in 1928 using powerful German-built pumps in order to expose the Roman craft known to lie there. Two immense and lavishly decorated wooden ships were discovered for the first time, having defied the efforts of Alberti, Demarchi and Fusconi in the preceding centuries.

The Lake Nemi finds immediately elucidated features only half-glimpsed elsewhere. The planks of the two great ships had been fixed together with wooden tongues or tenons slotted into corresponding

In 1904 two dugouts were discovered when Lake Chalain in the Jura was artificially drained (top). The largest (9.35 metres – about 30 feet – long, top) was of oak and some 3500 years old (late Bronze Age). In 1925, soon after the Lake Nemi finds, the Swiss Paul Vouga went down in a barrel (above) to examine the Bronze Age lake dwellings of Cortaillod.

cavities or mortises – a widespread practice in classical times, further illustrated by ancient wrecks discovered afterwards in the Mediterranean. Two anchors in a good state of preservation were also found: one wooden and 5.5 metres (18 feet) long with a fixed lead stock; the other of iron cased in wood, 3.5 metres (11 feet) long with a movable lead stock. For the more chauvinistic Fascist Italy the discovery of the latter discredited the 19th-century British 'invention' of the 'Admiralty' anchor (an iron anchor with a movable stock).

The main contribution of the Lake Nemi vessels, although constructed for lake use, was that they revealed, in depth and at a stroke, the Roman methods of building ships, seagoing or otherwise. The partial drainage of the lake in 1928 led to the discovery in 1931 of two new wrecks (one 5 metres long – 16 feet – long, the other 9 metres – 30 feet), for a long time the only known examples of small craft from classical times.

It was a tremendous feat of engineering to refloat the two great Roman vessels at Lake Nemi, a project that had been studied since 1926. The first one to be retrieved (bottom) was 71.3 metres (234 feet) long. In four years of excavations, directed by the engineer Guido Ucelli, the water level of the lake had fallen 21 metres (70 feet) by using powerful pumps. An iron anchor cased in wood (below) was recovered. Over 3.5 metres (11 feet) long, it had a movable stock stamped with its weight: 1275 Roman pounds, about 400 kg (900 lbs).

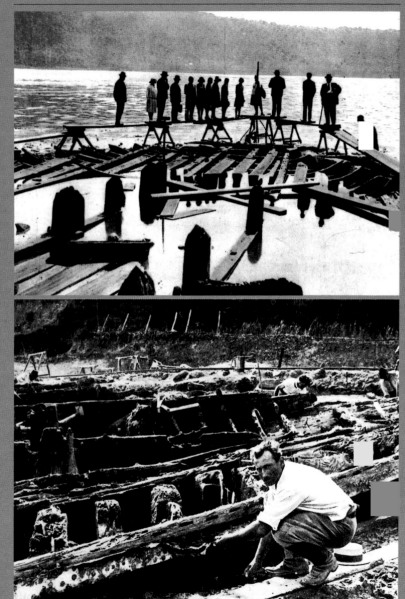

On 31 May 1944, during the Second World War, German troops retreating to the Italian Front set fire to the two great Roman ships at Lake Nemi that had been refloated two decades earlier. They were destroyed with the museum built for them on the lake shore. Six years later Guido Ucelli, who had directed the excavations in the lake, published *Le Navi di Nemi*, the most important book on the subject. It illustrated the retrieval of the first vessel from the water on 3 September 1929 (opposite above), its bronze lion and wolf heads (left), the lead sheathing of the hull (opposite below) – and the reconstruction of the ship (below) by the architect Ferrante and the sculptor Biondi that was shown at an exhibition in Rome in 1911.

The message from Alexandria

In 1916 Gaston Jondet, the French engineer in charge of enlarging the port of Alexandria in Egypt, published a survey of the artificial structures found under water. This ancient port had been the centre of a network that linked the Mediterranean, the Nile and the north lagoon in Egypt.

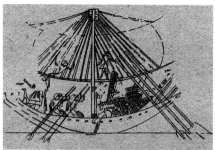

In the Bronze Age ships sailed all over the Mediterranean. The above drawing of an Egyptian vessel is copied from a 20th dynasty tomb (c. 1200–1085 BC) in Thebes.

Jondet saw the submarine structures as the remains of a gigantic port from the second millennium BC, opening a debate on whether Bronze Age sailors built ports. It was a particularly pertinent question because the number of Bronze Age objects found on various

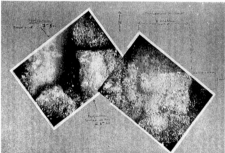

Mediterranean shores indicated that there had been widespread navigation offshore at the time. It therefore followed that seagoing vessels must have needed ports when they came into land.

In the 1930s Père André Poidebard made an important archaeological discovery under water on the Lebanese coast

Poidebard, a French Jesuit and archaeologist who was interested in the old Middle Eastern trade routes, used an aeroplane between 1925 and 1932 to look for traces of submerged remains. In 1934 he spotted,

Once an island, Tyre became a peninsula when Alexander the Great built a causeway to conquer it. It was an even earlier part of the port's history that was investigated in 1934 by the archaeologist and military chaplain Père Poidebard (opposite, far right), by taking aerial photographs above water (above left).

on photographs of the Lebanese coast, lighter patches in the roadsteads of Tyre, which he took to be underwater structures. Poidebard thought he had found the site of the Bronze Age port.

To examine the remains of what was possibly the ancient port, Poidebard hired divers equipped to take underwater photographs and personally supervised the operation through a glass-bottomed bucket held on the surface. The site was immense, bordered by two reefs forming a breakwater 550 metres (1800 feet) and 280 metres (900 feet) long by 30 metres (99 feet) wide. Despite using these methods, Poidebard had to admit that the survey was limited; and the divers asked to be accompanied by an engineer-diver who could identify the underwater forms they found.

A few years later the American Robert Braidwood found, near the 9th-century BC site of Tabbat el-Hammam on the Syrian coast, a wall without natural foundations. It was the first known artificial jetty, made of blocks fitted together, 200 metres (660 feet) long by 15 metres (50 feet) wide, and standing in 4 metres (about 13 feet) of water, enough to hold deep-sea-going craft.

Poidebard (below) used aerial photography in Lebanon, a technique employed by Paul Vouga as early as 1927 to observe the submerged remains of the Swiss lake settlements. It was after flying over the port of Tyre that Poidebard first began his study of the ancient harbour, tackling questions that had long remained unanswered. Between 1934 and 1936 he devoted himself to three survey operations, entrusting the identification of structures located from the air to divers.

In 1935 he used a glass-bottomed bucket to see and photograph below the surface (opposite, centre right: stone blocks 7.80 metres – 25 feet – deep in the south roadsteads of Tyre). At the end of 1935 the divers used a small 9.5 mm movie camera in a watertight case, changing to a Leica camera (see diver, far left) in 1936. Poidebard stated in 1937: 'The sole object of our investigation was to establish a method.'

The Gagnan-Cousteau breakthrough

At the World Fair in Paris in 1937 divers demonstrated in an aquarium the aqualung invented by Commandant Le Prieur, using a simple bottle of compressed air with a manually controlled supply.

Six years later, at the behest of Commandant Jacques-Yves Cousteau, the engineer Emile Gagnan invented a pressure regulator that enabled air to be supplied on demand to a diver carrying a tank of compressed air. In 1946 the aqualung (or scuba – <u>s</u>elf-<u>c</u>ontained <u>u</u>nderwater <u>b</u>reathing <u>a</u>pparatus), was made available to the public. For the first time divers could move freely under water with no impediment other than the air tank that they would now carry on their backs. The freedom of movement provided by the Cousteau-Gagnan aqualung was to lead to the discovery of many sites on the Mediterranean coast and in lakes such as Annecy and Bourget. Divers could now establish the precise topography of the piles of the lake dwellings sunk in the sediment, the key to the history of their inhabitants.

Left: twin tanks from scuba diving gear. The aqualung proved highly successful, with 25,000 models sold worldwide by 1955. Flippers and a face mask completed the equipment of those who were at last to open the doors of human history under water.

A public massacre

In 1943 a Danish diver examined a medieval wreck (a cog) in Kolding Fjord for the National Museum of Copenhagen. At the same time dozens of other wrecks from various periods were recorded in the dried-up Zuiderzee in Holland. What should be done with this flood of remains?

For one large vessel, judged to be of no interest as it had been built too recently (in 1800), the answer was destruction. The ship *Duguay-Trouin* had been captured by the British in 1805 at the battle of Trafalgar and renamed the *Implacable* by the Royal Navy. In 1949 it was still afloat, empty and bulky, in Portsmouth harbour. The Royal Navy decided to

destroy it and informed the French. The *Implacable* was towed out into the English Channel and powder charges were lit, with little success; in the end the vessel had to be sunk by the tugs.

The destruction of an old battleship, even a wooden one 150 years old, is a major operation. At its thickest the hull of a vessel such as the *Duguay-Trouin* was like an oak wall 80 cm (31 inches) thick. Although the old ship was in poor condition, it was still afloat, but its fate was decided on the grounds that it was causing an obstruction to the Royal Navy and was no longer of interest to the French. Having been towed 45 km (28

In 1950, off Albenga, southwest of Genoa, the Italian government archaeologist Nino Lamboglia tackled a very large 1st-century BC Roman merchant ship, the remains of which were caught now and then in fishing nets some 40 metres (130 feet) deep. The Albenga wreck, one of the giant Roman cargo carriers, contained thousands of amphorae, nearly all of the Dressel 1 form (see page 33), and was capable

miles) off the Sussex coast (above and below) into the Channel on its last voyage (top), the ship took two and a half hours to sink on 2 December 1949. Precedents had already been set: in Canada the *Lyman M. Davis*, the last tall ship of the Great Lakes, built in 1873, was burned publicly the night of 29 June 1934 near Toronto. At the time there was a great outcry, with one observer calling the destruction an act of rampant vandalism worthy of Nero.

of carrying over ten thousand. The Sorima salvage company offered its services free – a favour for which the archaeologist was to pay dearly. Throughout the month of February 1950 Lamboglia watched, powerless to do anything, as wine amphorae two thousand years old were shoved by the dozen on a cable or heaped into the metal jaws of a dredge bucket. The way in which the contents of the wreck were mishandled taught the archaeologist a lesson.

The statue of an actor below was among the bronzes rescued from the Mahdia wreck. They were meant for a temple, whose marble columns were the most visible part of the wreck. In 1948 the French GERS team (below) spent thirty-two hours diving for this cargo.

At the first underwater archaeology conference held at Cannes in 1955 Lamboglia gave a report on the objects salvaged from the sea at Albenga, speaking of a 'massacre of amphorae'. A member of the audience remarked that his tone was 'nostalgic'.

Excavation is not and never has been simply about gathering objects

Despite its failures of method, the Albenga project marked a turning-point: for the first time an archaeologist had taken an interest in a wreck for its historical value rather than its fortuitous discovery or its artistic contents.

From the date indicated by its amphorae, the Albenga wreck represented a key link in the history of Roman maritime trade. Lamboglia's experience proved that helmet divers and a dredge bucket were unable to carry out the necessary decoding underwater.

The French team's work on the Mahdia wreck took the aqualung out of the world of sport into the realm of research.

Pioneers in the field continued to break new ground. From 1946 to 1950 Poidebard was in Sidon, a site even older than Tyre, where the divers were equipped with an underwater camera. At Mahdia, in Tunisia, divers using aqualungs dug inside the hold of the ship that had lain forgotten since 1913, with 26 metres (85 feet) of its keel still extant.

Wrecks continued to be discovered in the early 1950s, almost always by amateurs strongly drawn to the clear waters of the Mediterranean. In France the Club Alpin Sous-marin distinguished itself by its work in eastern Provence. In the United States a group of increasingly active divers operated from California.

Very soon, despite the unsystematic character of the samples taken, the ancient wrecks found by these amateurs came to merit a chapter of their own in archaeological history: the wrecked cargos yielded tens, hundreds and even thousands of artefacts of

Digging at the Mahdia wreck in the early 1900s, Alfred Merlin's divers found a layer of wood (the deck) and under it objects of art. In 1948 the GERS team (Groupe d'Etudes et de Recherches Sous-marines) continued research on the wreck, raising column shafts (above left and right) and two lead anchor stocks of 700 kg (1550 lbs). In 1954 and 1955, the Tunisian Club of Undersea Studies reached the keel and cut off a 4 metre (13 foot) section to examine the hull, which was sheathed in lead and assembled with tenons and mortises.

a single type, often intact. Most importantly, the objects in each wreck were all contemporaneous with it, or no more than a few years older.

In 1950, when the 'amphora rush' had just begun in the Mediterranean, members of a Swedish diving club in Göteborg led by Jerker Lundell questioned local people and drew up an inventory of underwater remains off the coast of Bohuslän. The Swedes were alone in taking such pioneering steps; it was nearly half a century before the idea of an inventory of the underwater heritage became established.

In 1957 Commandant Tailliez, who was in charge of excavating the 1st-century BC Titan wreck (below) that had been discovered in 1948 off the Ile du Levant, retrieved over 700 amphorae, most of the Dressel 12 form. Tailliez experienced the problems of an archaeological operation.

The puzzle of Grand Congloué

At the Cannes conference in 1955 Fernand Benoît, who was responsible for antiquities on the coast of Provence, gave a report on the work carried out on a Roman wreck by Cousteau and his divers aboard the ship *Calypso*. The site was located off Marseilles at the submerged foot of a rocky cliff on the little island of Grand Congloué. Cristianini, the diver who reported the wreck after a decompression accident in October 1950, had talked of seeing 'jars' there. Launched in 1952, the operation was a logistical success to which the air lift, a tube 120 mm (nearly 5 inches) in diameter, made a vital contribution. A large quantity of ceramics – nearly 2000 amphorae, dishes

The air lift (above, at Grand Congloué), used to remove sediment by means of a jet of compressed air, came into general use from 1950.

and lamps – was raised. Fernand Benoît, the site archaeologist, was excited about the discovery of 7500 pieces of Campanian pottery. He had found traces of the same pottery on land on the coast, particularly near Marseilles. But he was not a diver.

The lead stock brought up by the GERS team (above) was part of an anchor of the type found at Lake Nemi twenty years earlier. These forms were to become familiar to Mediterranean divers.

As more and more finds were brought up, Benoît became more and more confused. An interval of a century (ranging from the late 3rd/early 2nd century BC to the late 2nd/early 1st century BC) separated the artefacts recovered. It was as if the ship had rested for a century between two cargos. Re-examining the excavation data and rereading Benoît's notebooks decades later, the French archaeologist Luc Long confirmed what his colleague and others working with him at the time had suspected: there were two wrecks, not one, below the submerged foot of the Grand Congloué cliff. Had Benoît not realized this?

Archaeologists under water: a notable absence

In fact, Benoît had been aware of the problem. Commandant Philippe Tailliez, an aqualung pioneer who took part in the investigations, related that during the 1953 operation a prototype of an underwater television camera had been used: 'On board the *Calypso*, the technicians and archaeologists watched from their armchairs as the divers moved among the amphorae.' As the end of the excavations approached in 1958, Benoît informed the second International Congress in Underwater Archaeology at Albenga: 'We know, from experience on the *Calypso*, how difficult it is precisely to establish and chart the distances and the position of wrecks and isolated objects.'

After a season of excavations on another ancient wreck near the Ile du Levant off the coast of Provence, Tailliez concluded: 'If an archaeologist had accompanied us to the bottom, he would have noted the precise position of each object before it was removed…he would have gathered, from examination *in situ*, imperceptible clues and more information.' Progress was made in 1958 when Lamboglia's team introduced a metal grid to mark the area of the excavation site, a technique adapted for lakes, using a triangular frame, two years later. Archaeologists were at last able to work *in situ*, under water.

Cousteau, advised by Benoît, set up the first great underwater archaeological worksite at Grand Congloué in 1952 (opposite bottom). Among the objects raised were thousands of pieces of Campanian pottery: bowls stuck together (opposite top); pottery with its glaze preserved by the sand (opposite centre).

In 1958, a year after the closure of the Grand Congloué site, Benoît (above) wrote: 'The excavation of an underwater site is not about fishing for amphorae.'

The grand-scale bungling at Albenga and the confusion at Grand Congloué were largely due to the absence of archaeologists at the underwater site. However, it was the lack of analytical tools that most hampered those who first had to handle the deluge of finds following the invention of the aqualung. The most blatant area of neglect was the ship itself: a container overlooked in favour of its contents.

CHAPTER 4

A NEW LOOK AT OLD SHIPS

With the exception of period models such as the miniature on the right, dating from the mid-15th century, that originally came from the Catalan shrine at Mataró, 19th-century marine archaeologists reconstructing vanished ships had to make do, in the words of the French archaeologist André Jal, 'with bits of debris from wrecks and pieces of text'. The invention of the aqualung gave humankind wide access to the nautical past. The diver on the left is placing markers on the wreck of the *Mauritius*, whose hold contained 18,000 ingots – 122 tonnes – of zinc.

The hulls of old reappear

A wreck of a ship from antiquity was first found in 1864 during work carried out at the site of the old port in Marseilles. This 'Caesar's galley', only fragments of which remain, was a Roman merchant vessel from the 2nd or 3rd century AD. Twenty years later 4th-century BC slipways used for launching triremes (warships with three banks of oarsmen) were discovered during excavations at Piraeus. Measuring 37 metres (121 feet) long by 5.5 metres (18 feet) wide, they settled part of a long debate about the maximum size of craft.

In August 1911 a case 12 metres (39 feet) in length and 10 tonnes in weight containing a Roman wreck made of oak was pulled across London by horse (below). Features such as the floor timbers (crosspieces on the hull bottom) and the complex joints in a section of planking indicated that the shell of the hull (below left) had been built before the frame had been laid. Examination of the wood later revealed that the ship dated from the 3rd century and had been built in northern Europe.

During the construction of County Hall in London in 1910 the remains of a Roman ship were found in the old bed of the Thames under 4.2 metres (nearly 14 feet) of mud. An unsuccessful attempt was made to protect the wood of the wreck exposed to the open air by coating it with glycerine. This was the first time a Roman wreck was studied in detail. Comparison of the hull with those of ancient wrecks found later showed the extent of the Mediterranean influence on the English Channel.

In 1930 a completely different type of wreck was found buried at Utrecht in Holland. Perhaps because of the then very recent discoveries at Lake Nemi, the Utrecht vessel was initially thought to be of the Roman period. Much later, carbon-14 tests dated it from the 8th century AD or thereabouts. The ship was found in an old bed of the Rhine sealed soon after AD 860. However, what was interesting about the Utrecht hull was not merely its date: very sturdy, the vessel was 18 metres (about 57 feet) long by some 4 metres (12 feet) wide; it lacked both a stem and a stern, and in place of a keel there was a wide, hollowed, oak bottom plank. The sides were raised with planks placed in parallel, which made the ship a form of extended dugout, contemporary with the Viking sailing ships but archaic by comparison.

The late medieval cog (above), dated c. 1380, found in Bremen in 1962, shows how northern Europe and the Mediterranean influenced each other. This type of partly clinker-built Hanse vessel, with its single mast, flat bottom and straight stern and prow, which appeared in the 12th century, was adopted in the Mediterranean and led to the large cargo ships.

The Vikings return

Traces of Vikings surfaced at Borre in Norway in about 1850, when roadworkers found the remains of a boat under gravel and sand in what had been the centre of a funerary mound. The vessel itself had vanished like a ghost, though the few objects that were recovered made it possible to date the site to around the year 900.

Other finds followed in quick succession. One of crucial importance to future underwater archaeology in fact occurred on land. A long – 22 metres (about 72 feet) – narrow vessel, some five hundred years older than the Viking period, was discovered at Nydam in Denmark in 1863. It was a clinker-built rowing boat, made of oak, fragile and with a low freeboard, and had no keel.

Funerary vessels found at the entrance to the Oslo

Built completely of oak, the 9th-century Gokstad ship (23.4 by 5.2 metres – 76 by 17 feet) was primarily designed for sailing, though it could be rowed by thirty-two oarsmen. In 1893, thirteen years after it was discovered, twelve Norwegians left Bergen on a replica (below) and crossed the Atlantic in forty-four days. As no Norwegian oak was large enough, the 25-metre (82-foot) keel was made from Canadian oak.

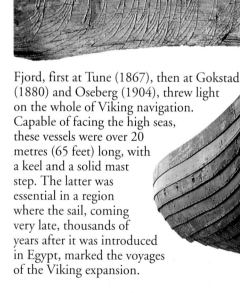

Fjord, first at Tune (1867), then at Gokstad (1880) and Oseberg (1904), threw light on the whole of Viking navigation. Capable of facing the high seas, these vessels were over 20 metres (65 feet) long, with a keel and a solid mast step. The latter was essential in a region where the sail, coming very late, thousands of years after it was introduced in Egypt, marked the voyages of the Viking expansion.

The discovery of a new type of hull made of limewood, 17 metres (about 55 feet) long, at Hjörtspring in south Denmark in 1921, immediately raised questions about the roots of shipbuilding in Scandinavia. Much older than previous examples – dating from 350–300 BC at the latest – the ship was distinctively made of overlapping

While the Gokstad vessel was a powerful sailing ship, the hull (bottom) dug up some 20 km (13 miles) away at Oseberg was a little older and less seaworthy. Built for thirty oarsmen, the ship became a woman's burial place around AD 800.

wooden planks sewn together. This method of assembly showed how the northern craftsmen of twenty-three centuries ago, using planks cut from tree trunks, had found a way of producing a ship much larger than any tree used in its construction. Examined in this way, the ship was a virtual dugout expanded from a mother tree-trunk that had not been large enough to meet the seafaring ambitions of her offspring.

A fleeting imprint

From 1933 to 1934, when the old harbour at Kalmar in Sweden was drained, the archaeologist Harald Åkerlund excavated some twenty wrecks dating from 1250 to 1650. At the time only wrecks that dated to at least the Middle Ages interested archaeologists in Europe. The 17 metre-long (55-foot) gunboat *Philadelphia*, a national symbol in America, was treated differently. She was found intact in 1935 and raised. She had sunk in Lake Champlain in 1776 during the American War of Independence.

Another important step forward was taken with the excavation in 1939 of an Anglo-Saxon ship burial in sand at Sutton Hoo near Woodbridge in Suffolk. The site originally contained two Anglo-Saxon ships, one of which had survived with its wood intact. The other, larger, vessel, which was excavated with meticulous care despite the total lack of wood, had only left in the sand an impression, from which its form could be re-created. Later it was suggested that the ship could have been fitted with a mast and a large square sail. Sutton Hoo represents an intermediate stage between the discoveries from the first centuries AD, such as the Nydam ship, and the great Viking sites, such as Gokstad, where the rowing boat, fitted this time with a sturdy keel, has become a sailing ship of the high seas.

At Sutton Hoo archaeologists studied a virtual object (above): all that remained of the largest ship (27 metres – 89 feet long) from this 7th-century royal tomb was an impression in the sand. Skilled excavation work revealed that it had a thick central plank, on either side of which were nine strakes.

Underwater archaeology became a scientific discipline with decisive initiatives in the late 1950s

Most of the credit must be taken, at sea, by a handful of Americans and Scandinavians. Armed only with a metal core sampler (a simple weighted and sharpened tube that extracted a piece of whatever it hit) and the conviction that the cold and not very salty Baltic water would preserve wood in wrecks, the Swedish engineer Anders Franzén set about looking for the *Vasa*, a large warship that had sunk in 30 metres (100 feet) of water on her maiden voyage in 1628 outside Stockholm. In 1956, after several years of probing the mud from a small boat, Franzén was at last rewarded when he found a piece of oak with his core sampler. The largest archaeological project in naval and underwater history had just begun.

Nearly 70 metres (300 feet) in total length, the *Vasa* (below) sank on her maiden voyage in 1628, along with 64 cannons and 50 out of the 437 men. The masts were 52 metres (170 feet) tall and carried nearly 1200 square metres (13,000 square feet) of sail – too much, perhaps, as the *Vasa* heeled over in a squall, flooded and then sank. The disaster raised questions about the ship's stability at the

REGALSKEPPET "WASA"
1628

time and the shipwright was brought to trial. When the wreck was discovered in 1956 Franzén (left) won nationwide support for the project and set in motion an outstanding salvage operation.

That same year two amateur divers reported to the National Museum in Copenhagen that they had found ancient clinker-built wrecks in the Roskilde Fjord, near the village of Skuldelev. The water was very shallow (between 50 cm and 3 metres – between 20 inches and 10 feet) and, at the beginning, diving was used as a training exercise in underwater archaeological techniques. After three diving operations (from 1957 to 1959) the archaeologists decided to construct a steel cofferdam around the wrecks, so that the area could be pumped empty. Six ships (which later turned out to be only five) were then identified. The excavation revealed

After a cofferdam (below) was erected at the Roskilde Fjord site in May and June of 1962, and water pumped out, excavation work in the mud (bottom) continued for fifteen weeks.

the consummate skill of the 11th-century carpenters who varied the same basic model to construct both merchant and warships. Yet again sails and rigging, the most vulnerable elements, were missing from the archaeological site. However, it was established that the vessels had a more rigid frame than those of the preceding period – the supple craft that had crossed the sea with the grace of swans in the great days of Viking expansion.

At the same period, the Americans applied lessons learned in Scandinavia to the Mediterranean

Resuming in the late 1950s the research started by Greek divers at Antikythera in 1900, the American Peter Throckmorton found a vital and overlooked piece of evidence in the National Museum in Athens, fifty years after the cargo containing works of art had been recovered: the shipwrecked vessel. Nothing remained but minute pieces of wood that showed the planking had been assembled with wooden tenons and mortises, a technique already visible in 1864 in 'Caesar's galley' found at Marseilles and in 1910 at County Hall.

The birth of underwater archaeology as a science owes much to the New York diver and sailor Peter Throckmorton, who was an anthropologist by training. In 1958, when he was thirty years old, he spent several months diving off the Turkish coast with Kemal Arras, the captain of a sponge boat, who showed him some one hundred shipwrecks. Throckmorton's interest was aroused by one in particular, which

Throckmorton had learned of the existence of many ancient wrecks from Turkish sponge divers. Recognizing the enormous archaeological potential of these sites, he took steps to have them investigated. George Bass, a specialist in the Middle East at the University of Pennsylvania Museum, was the first land archaeologist to learn to dive in order to study in person an underwater site off Cape Gelidonya (Cape of the Swallows) in Turkey, about

lay 27 metres (90 feet) off Cape Gelidonya. Back in the United States, Throckmorton contacted the young archaeologist George Bass (above, with his wife, in 1960 at Cape Gelidonya). Kemal's wreck turned out to be thirty-one centuries old. The rest is history.

which Throckmorton had written. The excavation of 1960 brought to light the bronze cargo of a Phoenician trading ship and greatly contributed to the study of the Bronze Age in the east Mediterranean. Of the ship itself, however, little remained and for their next excavation in 1961 the Turkish-American Bass team headed to the little island of Yassi Ada, off which Turkish sponge divers had located a number of ancient wrecks, to excavate a 7th-century Byzantine ship. The wreck, whose wooden parts were still extant, lay between 37 and 43 metres (120 and 140 feet) deep.

It was here that the Scandinavian school came

While research in the early 1960s had defined two different approaches to ancient shipbuilding – the 'shell-first' technique (illustrated in the first drawing on the left), with no prebuilt inner frame, and the 'frame-first' technique (opposite top) which started with the frame – archaeologists later observed that some ships were made by a 'mixed' method. The large 1st-century BC merchant vessel found at Madrague de Giens, France (bottom left), provided just such an example: its shell-first construction (as reconstructed in the vertical series of drawings to the left) showed that some floor timbers had been fixed to the keel, actively contributing to the strength of the whole as in a frame-first type of vessel.

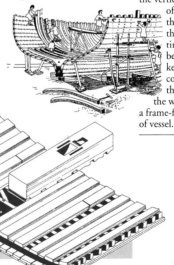

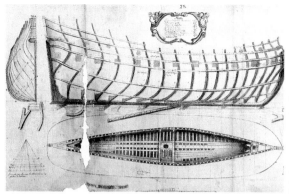

The archaeologist's task in tracing technical advances and influences is made more difficult by the fact that ships travel. From the 17th century onwards precise drawings provide valuable information – on the left is a Dutch-inspired plan of a French 'flute' of 1684. Such precision was unknown in earlier illustrations. The model immediately below is of a late 16th-century wreck excavated in the port of Calvi in Corsica. The flat transom stern with gunports and a compact frame evokes the shapes found in the period pictures of ships.

into its own, notably with the work of pioneers such as Olof Hasslöf, who distinguished two types of wooden craft: those built on to a primitive skeleton, the frame, which was later covered with hull planks; and those whose shell was built first, with a smooth hull inside and outside and an inner frame or ribs added only at the end in order to strengthen it. The oldest ships – the Roman wrecks, for example – were constructed on the 'shell-first' principle, while the others were of the 'frame-first' type.

An outline strategy for excavating a wreck

The Bass team, in association with the Bodrum Museum in Turkey, was largely responsible for this change of approach. The 7th-century wreck at Yassi Ada was important in representing a transitional stage between the two shipbuilding

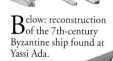

Below: reconstruction of the 7th-century Byzantine ship found at Yassi Ada.

methods, being built shell-first at the bottom and frame-first at the top. From now on the choice of excavation sites made by archaeologists from the American Institute of Nautical Archaeology was to be determined by the ship. The next site, Serçe Liman, where Turkish sponge divers had found 11th-century amphorae, was chosen because further information was needed on the end of the 'shell-first' method in the eastern Mediterranean. Excavation showed

The question of ship construction methods is central to excavations that differ on the technical front. Above left is the excavation site of the 11th-century wreck at Serçe Liman in Turkey, where work began in 1972; above right, its reconstruction based on remains: 15 metres (nearly 50 feet) long on deck, 5.1 metres (16 feet) at the beam (the broadest point) with a flat bottom. Left is the Roman wreck known as *Blackfriars I*, excavated in 1963 in a steel cofferdam in the middle of the Thames. Made of oak, the ship, which was 16.5 metres (about 55 feet) long by 6.6 metres (about 22 feet) wide, had a flat bottom, no keel but strong floor timbers. The bottom and sides were built using two distinct methods, illustrating a type of construction known as 'Romano-Celtic'.

the Serçe Liman ship to be of the 'frame-first' type.

Analysis of other remains, such as those belonging to an ancient tug (2nd–3rd century) found in 1962 in the Thames at Blackfriars in London showed that in practice variants and intermediate methods had existed, sometimes concurrently. The Belgian naval archaeologist Lucien Basch stressed the 'active' or 'passive' role of the ship's inner frame. Details that had previously passed unnoticed, such as the direction used to drive wooden treenails into the planking, were noted from now on. Beyond academic debates, a new way of interpreting wrecks was born.

The chance discovery in 1985 of a very early 17th-century Dutch wreck, the *Mauritius*, off Cape Lopez in Gabon was an actual example of something that was already known from documents: in the lower part of the hull in large vessels the Dutch had retained construction techniques of the 'shell-first' type. The study of the remains of the hull, preserved over a surface of some 65 square metres (700 square feet), was now considered so important that it relegated the cargo to second place.

Apart from the richness and variety of the cargo, the excavation of the *Mauritius* (below) concentrated on the details of the the hull's method of construction. The ship, built from 1601 to 1602 and wrecked on its return from Asia in 1609, displayed characteristic features of the Dutch shipyards, which, at the time of the first voyages to the East made by the Dutch East India Company, preserved methods in which the lower part of the hull was built without first fitting an inner cross-frame.

Aconference held in Miami in 1985 established the idea of a wet site archaeology dealing with artefacts saturated in water, such as those found in marshes. Whether shipwrecks belong in this category is still under discussion. Some suggest the following dividing line: on one side, 'mobile' objects, such as ships; on the other, fixed structures, such as ports and submerged dwellings.

CHAPTER 5

THE LAWS OF SINKING

This entirely man-made Iron Age stone jetty seen from the air (opposite) is the earliest one known of its kind. It was built in the 9th century BC at Tabbat el-Hammam, on the Syrian coast. The hand from a bronze statue (right) was found in the Adriatic, off Brindisi.

Since the late 1950s underwater archaeologists have demonstrated that excavating a vessel, on land or in water, is based on common principles: the only relevant criterion, all things considered, is the relationship between the object being investigated and the water that surrounds it. From the original confusion, archaeologists will work out within this specific physical environment a chronological framework in which the shipwreck is given a prominent place.

Presented as a 'time capsule', where history has been frozen since the moment of the sinking, the wreck has the same properties in the archaeologist's eyes as the stratum from a disaster on land. Life comes to a halt at a precise instant as a ship sinks, just

Some shipwrecks underwent intensive salvage operations almost immediately after they sank. In the

above painting divers are rescuing the cargo of the *San Pedro de Alcántara*, which sank on the coast of Peniche in Portugal in 1786 on its return voyage from Peru. Left: the wreck of the *Conde de Tolosa*, which sank at Santo Domingo with a cargo from Spain.

as it does when a volcano erupts or a town is burnt. Rarely did anything exceed the duration of the final voyage other than the ship itself, the sailors' equipment and luxury cargos, such as the bronze statues at Anti-kythera, which were already several centuries old when they sank in the 1st century BC.

It is easier to establish the date of the sinking than the date of the ship itself

Modern statistics show a strong relationship between aged vessels and accidents at sea. It may be that the entire history of the merchant navy, including the

Coins can provide valuable information on the precise date when domestic goods ('treasure') were abandoned or a cargo was sunk. The gold and silver coins on the left are from the wreck of the *Tolosa*, which sank in 1724. It is more difficult to establish a date where a single coin is found, as it could be much older than the vessel. The same problem also occurs with collections of works of art, such as that found in 1928 near Cape Artemision in Greece, from which came the 2nd-century BC bronze horse and rider (below).

vessels of antiquity, was affected by a similar phenomenon. The age of a sailing vessel can sometimes be determined from the coin that shipwrights, observing an old custom, used to put near the cavity of the mast step. In such cases it is necessary to discover whether the coin, which can be accurately dated thanks to a vast accumulated body of numismatic knowledge, was already an antique when the vessel was built.

Modern methods of dating have contributed

additional tools, of varying precision, to help establish the age of a vessel. Developed at the end of the Second World War, carbon-14 dating allows the age of organic materials at an archaeological site to be determined. However, in addition to its initial inaccuracy – a margin of several decades in antiquity, much more for the last moments of the wooden sailing vessels – when applied to wood from a ship the carbon-14 technique is necessarily dealing with a material that was already old when the tree was chopped down and the vessel was built.

Dendrochronology, based on analysis of the annual rings of trees, whose thickness alters according to the climatic variations of the particular region, makes it possible to date the felling of a tree to the nearest year, provided that its outer layers have been preserved.

The technique does, however, require some knowledge of the wood's origin – rarely available in the case of an unidentified maritime shipwreck.

Maritime trade: ship versus ox-cart

The preponderance of shipwrecks over other underwater sites at sea is first due to the inaccessibility for hundreds of years of the remains of sunken vessels, which are protected by a deep layer of water – unlike ruins on land.

The aqualung broke into this historical cocoon like a fox into a henhouse. In 1979 archaeologists from Bristol University led by A. J. Parker recorded 660 Mediterranean sites from antiquity and the Middle Ages, taking the inventory up to the year 1500. The number rose to 1189 in 1992, referring this time to the wreck sites from the Black Sea and the north-western European coast.

The pre-eminence of wreck sites also reflects the sheer volume of sea trade throughout history. The French historian Gustave Glotz has recorded that tiles could be transported in ancient Greece between

Examination of the annual growth rings of an oak tree (above) from a dugout found in Lake Chalain in the Jura in 1904 made it possible to give a date of pre-959 BC, determined from a master chronology established in neighbouring regions.

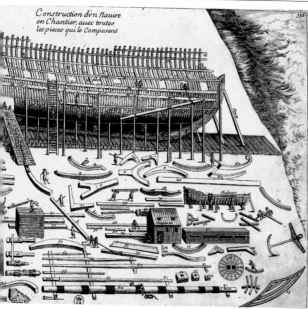

Construction d'vn nauire en Chantier, auec toutes les pieces qui le Composent

The ship played a major role in the history of trade because it could carry large quantities of merchandise in the hold. When a ship sinks, its contents, as well as the vessel itself, are dispersed according to phenomena – currents and marine organisms, for example – that differ from those occurring on land. The 17th-century engraving on the left shows the construction of a vessel of the period with some of its component parts.

Below: the shipwreck that took place at Kyrenia in Cyprus 2300 years ago. Analysis of material from the hull showed the ship to have been nearly a century old when it sank.

Lakiadai and Eleusis at a cost of 40 drachmas overland and eight times less by the Corinth boat, although the distance covered was three times as long.

Falling bodies: an exception to the rule

A wreck is a foreign body deposited at the bottom of the sea by accident, and divers have observed phenomena that have overturned some of the principles established for land archaeology. There were deviations from the law of gravity.

In the 1960s the diver Alexander McKee renewed the search, 120 years after the Deane brothers, for the wreck of the *Mary Rose*, which had sunk off Portsmouth in 1545. He observed a remarkable phenomenon: such was the suction created by local currents next to a sunken hull that a ditch had been carved around it. All kinds of objects carried by the

current then became trapped in this artificial cavity, creating 'horizontal' contamination and offering little scope for stratigraphy, a highly reliable tool of land archaeology adapted from 19th-century geologists and used to re-create the history of a place by examining its earth strata.

The reason why this method does not work everywhere under water – fresh or salt – has to do with the nature of the site. Stratigraphy has meaning only on sedentary sites where human beings have deposited the remains of their lives, with each layer being pressed down by successive generations. The shipwreck, a nomad paralysed in mid-journey, does not come into this category.

Examination of strata on a site allows its history to be traced. In the photograph (below left) of a stratigraphic section from the basement of a submerged dwelling near Zurich vertical wooden posts and darker layers indicating occupation are separated by light areas of sterile sediment. At the Colònia de Sant Jordi anchorage in the Balearic Islands two layers of amphorae separated by 20 cm (8 inches) of sterile sand had built up in the two centuries between two ancient shipwrecks (drawing, below). The more recent (the upper layer) went back to the 1st century AD, the time of the emperors Claudius or Nero.

At anchor between two winds

In contrast to the 'closed' time-span of a wreck, sites with an 'open' time-span consist of an accumulation of remains in one place over a long period of time. Anchorages are an undramatic but essential example

Unlike ports, anchorages were often cut off from the coast and had no links to the hinterland. They were temporary stopping places that gave

of archaeological sites where objects have accumulated in the same place over different periods. An anchorage is a protected location where, in the absence of a port, sailing ships come to drop anchor and seek shelter from wind and sea. The remains found there consist of debris thrown overboard or objects, particularly anchors, accidentally left behind.

An anchorage has neither the chronological virtues of a wreck nor the vertical sequence of layers found in a stratigraphic site, with one exception: being an open place where shelter can suddenly be removed by a sharp change in wind direction, an anchorage sometimes contains many wrecks piled one on top of the other. Digging in the sterile sand and seaweed on the bed of the anchorage at the Colònia de Sant Jordi on the south coast of Majorca, underwater excavators discovered two quite distinct layers, which corresponded to two ancient wrecks.

shelter to passing vessels, often over centuries. Above is a small anchorage on the Italian coast today.

Stone remains silent

Half anchorage, half port, the oldest harbour sites in Lebanon, studied after Poidebard by the English archaeologist Honor Frost in the 1960s, revived the question raised by the engineer Gaston Jondet in Alexandria at the beginning of the century: were ports built in the Bronze Age?

Nicholas Flemming, a British geologist specializing in old harbour structures, has declared that 'finds of Bronze Age artificial harbours are as scarce as hen's teeth'.

Adopting the Poidebard air surveying method, but supplementing it with the aqualung, Frost made a survey from 1963 to 1964 of the ancient structures carved out of the rock at Arwad, a small, bare island

The first ports made use of natural shelters that people gradually improved. For example, the line of reefs at Arwad, parallel to the Syrian coast, was used as a harbour by ships in the Bronze Age. The aerial view above, taken by Honor Frost, is of the eastern part of Arwad island. Frost has shown that jetties were carved from the rock, a common practice among the Phoenicians.

that had offered shelter on the Phoenician coast. Mentioned in an Egyptian source of the 15th century BC, the Arwad site and line of reefs up to the island of Machroud further south are situated off Tabbat el-Hammam.

At Tyre Frost felt that Poidebard, who had not actually dived himself to inspect the site, had mistaken for an old port what she interpreted as an old industrial quarter. In trying to give a precise date to the stone structures she examined under water, Frost, like Jondet, Poidebard and others before them, had difficulty appraising the material, which revealed little. There were no indicative details offering scope for analysis, such as the 'bond' of the stone construction, data available for later periods, to help reach a conclusion; and Poidebard before her had discovered stratigraphy to be inconclusive here. Frost concluded at this point that stratigraphy was unworkable under the sea.

At the end of the 1930s Robert Braidwood undertook a survey at Tabbat el-Hammam on the Syrian coast opposite the islet of Machroud, the southern limit of the shelter created by the line of reefs at Arwad. By dating the layers of occupation of the tells – mounds formed on land by accumulated ruins – Braidwood was able to date the great stone jetty of Tabbat el-Hammam (below), built in the 9th century BC. It replaced the port of Machroud whose structures were slowly sinking into the sea.

The harbours of antiquity

These first studies revealed the Phoenicians' skill in building harbours. They knew how to cut into rocks to adapt sites that were chosen in the first place for their naturally favourable features. In addition to simple quays, jetties and foundation trenches, the excavations at Carthage in 1974 brought to light another aspect of this specialized engineering: two basins cut in the rock and linked to the sea illustrated the technology of the 'cothon' – an artificial inner harbour carved out of the shore – that Poidebard had hoped to find in Tyre. Another practice of the Phoenicians was building a harbour at the mouth of a river. At Leptis Magna – which was originally Punic, but was later annexed by Rome in the 2nd century BC – on the coast of present-day Libya, a small water course thus silted up the harbour. The site, which was excavated on land in the 1930s by the Italians, comprised a 10 hectare (24 acre) basin with a passage 80 metres (260 feet) wide. Part of it is now under water. Recent French excavations have shown that the length of the quays at Leptis Magna,

In 1974 the archaeological excavations at Carthage in Tunisia brought to light two harbours carved out of the shore in Punic times. The first, reconstructed above, was used for merchant vessels, the second for warships.

formerly estimated at some 800 metres (2625 feet) and then 1200 metres (3930 feet), was in fact over 1500 metres (4920 feet), an indication of the importance of this early ancient harbour.

At Ostia, near Rome, the immense complex started by the Emperor Claudius in AD 42 north of the mouth of the Tiber and completed half a century later under the Emperor Trajan comprised two basins with a combined total surface of over 130 hectares (320 acres). Before the imperial port of Ostia was developed, the main harbour of Republican Rome lay far away from the capital at Puteoli (Pozzuoli) in the Bay of Naples. It was here that *pozzuolana*, a reddish volcanic powder that was employed by the Romans to make cement for use in the sea, began to be extracted.

In his *History of the Jewish War* the Jewish historian Flavius Josephus (37–?100) commented on the engineering skills involved in constructing the gigantic port of Sebastos in Caesarea in Palestine, completed in twelve years (22–10 BC) on the orders of King Herod on a low and narrow coast exposed to the winds.

Situated on the Libyan coast by the mouth of a wadi that later silted up, the harbour at Leptis Magna, whose ruins are shown below, was already thriving from the cereal trade when the native-born Emperor Lucius Septimius Severus improved the town and enlarged the port to ten times its original size in the 2nd century. At its apogee the following century Leptis Magna had nearly a hundred thousand inhabitants.

Herod and plate tectonics

In 1975, at the behest of the Israel Electric Company that was looking into setting up a nuclear power station, the archaeologist Avner Raban and his colleagues at Haifa University examined the underwater structures of Herod's port to evaluate the movements of the substratum in the region. In two thousand years the ruins of the old port had sunk 5–6 metres (16–20 feet) under the sea, while at Athlit, 30 kilometres (18 miles) north, no movement was detected. The object was to establish whether the rectilinear form of the eastern Mediterranean coast was or was not due to a break in the continental shelf at that spot. Directed by Avner Raban, the divers found evidence that the site of the port at Caesarea had gradually suffered subsidence and had probably been abandoned at the end of the 2nd century.

In the early 1990s Raban discovered under the water traces of huge wooden cases full of *pozzuolana*. But it was the amphorae from ships that had sunk above the remains of the old port in the 3rd and 4th centuries AD that enabled Raban and his divers to put a date on the gradual sinking of the great site. Not for the first time, wrecks played the part of chronological markers.

Geologists and submerged archaeological remains

The question of submerged archaeological remains has intrigued geologists for a long time. It is complicated because it involves two distinct phenomena: on the one hand, changes in sea-level brought about by the movement of continental plates along the sea shore and, on the other, the climatic variations that have affected the ice sheets around the polar regions.

At the beginning of this century the Greek Phokion Negris, a pioneer in studying monuments covered by the sea, attributed their submergence to

The aerial photograph (opposite) shows Herod's old port, Sebastos, built at the end of the 1st century BC on a low, straight piece of coast at the town of Caesarea in Israel. The extent of the constructions was uncovered by underwater excavations (opposite below). These investigations revealed traces of wooden caissons filled with hydraulic cement, which had been sunk *in situ* and which served as a foundation for the port structures. Objects found at the site, such as the late amphora below, have made it possible to study the progressive abandonment of the port.

a recent rise in sea-level. However, at Phalásarna in Crete a movement in the opposite direction, which had been noticed since the 19th century, raised the old shore: an old fish pond once exactly at sea-level – a precise piece of evidence – now lies 5 metres (16 feet) above the water.

In the early 1960s Nicholas Flemming, a geologist who was also a diver, made a detailed underwater study at Apollonia in Libya of old structures that had progressively been submerged. He brought to light, in shallow water, an inner harbour linked by a channel to an outer harbour, fortifications and ship sheds, whose dimensions (31 metres long by 6 wide – 100 by 20 feet) determined the size of the ships they could shelter. At the end of the 1980s French archaeologists embarked on a stratigraphic underwater excavation of dumps lying on the edge of the ancient port of Apollonia. Pottery

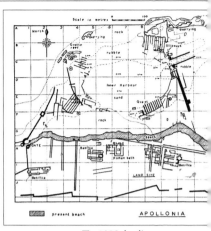

In 1985 the diver Henri Cosquer found, off the French coast, at a depth of 36 metres (118 feet), the entrance of a cave decorated by Upper Palaeolithic artists about 27,000 and 18,500 years ago.

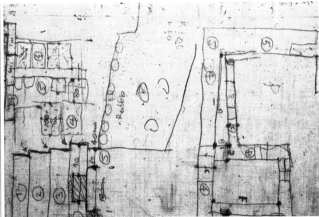

found within successive strata roughly a metre (three feet) thick made it possible to draw up a history of the site layer by layer. Spanning more than a thousand years from the 4th century BC to the arrival of the Arabs in the 7th century AD, the site was abandoned as the sea gradually took possession of the stones. It is now known that the continental shelf of Africa sinks in the north beneath that of Greece and the Balkans. The effect has been to bring about a rise in the water level of some 4 metres (13 feet) since the last days of antiquity and to submerge ancient coastal sites in Libya, such as Apollonia and Leptis Magna.

Geologists and archaeologists have long realized the advantages of working together on all sites at the edge of the sea, where the water level acts at one and the same time as a barrier and a witness. The benefits of teamwork apply equally to the study of the shore in the first days of navigation and to the study of prehistory, when humankind walked on what is now the sea floor. During the peak of glaciation in the Upper or Late Palaeolithic the sea-level was admittedly 120–125 metres (394–410 feet) lower than today. Therefore coastal sites and remains from that period lie within reach of divers and diving techniques.

Flemming's studies of the Apollonia site led him to conclude that the coast had subsided by several metres. With his team he identified two harbours, shown in his plan of the old port above left: one for merchant vessels, the other for warships; the shaded area represents the beach today. North of the beach, in the water, are the original foundations of the Greek town, on the mother rock. The drawing above, made on a formica sheet during a dive, shows the structures of the tower found in square C10 of the plan above left.

Baia, a drowned town

The first to use stratigraphy under water in a systematic manner were those excavating the bottoms of lakes, where the period concerned stretched from recent prehistory to medieval times.

At sea stratigraphy proved to be effective for studying sites such as the town of Baia near Naples, which had been submerged during an earthquake caused by a volcano. The old shoreline now lies some 400 metres (1300 feet) out to sea. In 1959 Lamboglia turned his attention to the underwater ruins at Baia and was to uncover cobbled streets and thermal buildings that had lain hidden under mud and seaweed. Twenty years later a large and richly decorated nymphaeum was excavated under the water very close by.

The nature and distribution of the layers of material found at Baia made it possible to date the abandonment of the site to the late 3rd century AD. Such was the tectonic activity of this volcanic region that some ancient monuments had first been submerged and had later resurfaced, only finally to be covered once more by water. Ironically the trading vessels that now call into the Bay of Baia scrape the ancient walls with their anchors. The ancient town has become a mooring ground.

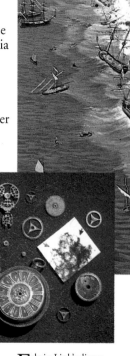

A city sunk by a wave: Port Royal

Shortly before noon on 7 June 1692 three consecutive tremors followed by a gigantic wave almost entirely destroyed the city of Port Royal in Jamaica with its 5000 inhabitants and 2000 buildings. It was only thanks to the research carried out in 1959 by the American underwater explorer Edwin Link,

Edwin Link's divers recovered the above watch at Port Royal. Its hands had entirely corroded but an X-ray showed they had stopped at 11:43, exactly when the earthquake destroyed the city.

R.V. Nicholson
National Geographic Staff

sponsored by the National Geographic Society and the Smithsonian Institution in Washington, D.C., that a plan of the town's ruins was made using ultrasonic soundings. Twenty-five years later the archaeologist D. L. Hamilton, who was in charge of a field school at the site, described the underwater ruins of a building: 'From architectural evidence it is clear that the northern three rooms were constructed first and utilized for a period of time before the southern three rooms were added.' The same reference to cardinal points serve the house builders of old and the archaeologists of today; not so with a wreck, a mobile object frozen by chance into its burial ground.

The above reconstruction shows the tidal wave that engulfed Port Royal. Concentrated in a few hectares (about 50 acres), the city was built mainly of brick. Nearly 2000 people lost their lives when two-thirds of it slid into the sea. In 1859 a Royal Navy diver identified the ruins of Fort James (on the bottom right of the illustration).

The large number of shipwrecks found in the early 1950s on the French Mediterranean coast were predominantly vessels from classical times. Underwater sites typically yielded amphorae or a cargo of rusted metal sheets. It was, to the divers' eyes, as if ships had suddenly vanished in late antiquity only to reappear in modern times.

CHAPTER 6
LUCK OR PERSISTENCE

The remains visible on the seabed can often be misleading: in the case of the Byzantine wreck known as *Yassi Ada I* (opposite), which lay in 36 metres (120 feet) of water, the cargo of 900 amphorae hid what was left of the ship – some ten per cent of its wood buried in the sand, the rest having been eaten by marine organisms. Right: wood eaten by shipworm, a watercolour of 1836 by John Deane.

The amphora

Of the two hundred shipwrecks on the French Mediterranean coast recorded in 1981, two-thirds dated from antiquity. Divers noticed a scarcity of wrecks after that period until the Renaissance. It is tempting to link the gap with the decline in Roman trade.

Some have challenged this interpretation on the grounds that wrecks with amphorae or cannons are easier to spot than those carrying more perishable, and therefore less visible, goods, such as leather wine skins and wooden barrels. For divers, the amphora has, like cannons, the advantage of its large size. Resistant, easy to spot, the amphora, a pottery container, has taken on a variety of shapes throughout history, making it easy to date. It is an effective 'calendar' of trade in antiquity. For example, the Dressel 1 form, found in many of the ancient wrecks in the French Mediterranean, was used for about a century while Italian wine was being exported to Gaul on a large scale. According to the archaeologist André Tchernia, the trade involved between 120,000 and 150,000 hectolitres a year, equivalent to a total of between 55 and 66 million amphorae being delivered to Gaul over a century.

These figures are consistent with the finds made by modern divers: forty-four wrecks with Dressel 1 amphorae were reported in the French Mediterranean at the beginning of the 1980s.

The barrel

Initially amphorae carried wine and olive oil, but later they were used for fish products, for which the Romans had developed a taste. Rome, an enormous city, also consumed huge quantities of wine, which, in the 2nd century, was supplied by Gaul in its own flat-bottomed amphorae. But from the 3rd century AD, when money was devalued, towns were depopulated, and economic life declined, amphora forms evolved more slowly, making it more difficult

A large container made of clay that does not perish in the sea, the amphora was used by all Mediterranean ships in antiquity. Since the late 19th century it has been studied in detail, on the basis of its shape (from left to right, are Dressel forms 1, 2 and 4 – see page 33). Nowadays amphorae tend to be identified more by their place of manufacture.

to date them. Wrecks from this time are rare: out of over a thousand recorded in the Mediterranean only fifty-four date from the 4th century. Is this just a coincidence? Far from it; Rome and then Byzantium was on the wane. Owing to an interruption or decline in seafaring, only a few of the wrecks found came from the Moslem Mediterranean, a tendency that continued until the beginning of the Renaissance.

However, wrecks with amphorae made from durable material and in shapes that are easier to spot under water might cause less visible, later or even contemporaneous wrecks to be overlooked. A simple vat initially designed for fermenting wine

In 1967 French naval divers found the remains of a 1st-century BC ship (below) at Madrague de Giens, near Toulon. Research on it answered many questions raised by a great amphora wreck, found at Albenga in 1950, concerning the great merchant vessels of that period, their construction and loading methods.

rather than transporting it, the barrel came to replace the amphora, though not in any uniform way either in terms of time or place. In Italy, for instance, the barrel began to take the place of the amphora from the 2nd and 3rd centuries AD and by the 4th century it was an everyday object in Rome. But in other regions the 'revolution' of the barrel did not occur until the Middle Ages.

With the appearance of artillery in the history of navigation, cannons, which are large, durable and easy to spot under water, provide a landmark for divers as effective as amphorae for more ancient times. Barrels and casks have then replaced the former pottery containers. Most importantly, the ships of the Renaissance have documentary records.

The vessel from Genoa

In April 1979 the diver Alain Visquis found traces of a great Renaissance ship in the bay of Villefranche-sur-Mer. The underwater excavations, which lasted eight years (from 1982 to 1990) under the direction of Commandant Max Guérout, revealed typically Mediterranean methods of construction and also the presence of gunports – the earliest to be found in a wreck. These remains, which lay under more than a metre (three feet) of mud, belonged to one of the powerful armed *navi* of Genoese trade, with high

The above bas-relief found at Cabrières d'Aygues, at the foot of the Lubéron, shows barrels and amphorae being used at the same time. The amphorae are flat-bottomed – Gaulish 4 (1–3rd centuries) – or encased in basketwork. The scene illustrates the decline of the amphora in late antiquity in favour of the more capacious and robust barrel.

hulls and raised sterns. Barrels and kegs found on the Villefranche wreck varied greatly in size, testifying to the arithmetical complexity of a cargo plan at the time, when only the skipper knew from experience how many *cantares*, *mine* of grain or *vegete* of wine or oil his *nave* could accommodate. Historical research suggests that the wreck excavated at Villefranche is the *Lomellina*, which was sunk in 1516. From now on archaeological excavation was linked with documentary evidence.

While a mound of amphorae is typical of an ancient wreck from the classical period in the Mediterranean, naval artillery, which was introduced at the end of the Middle Ages, is one of the most visible references for a diver to indicate a later wreck site (bottom left, a wrought-iron cannon).

Above: gun-carriage wheel from the *Lomellina* showing the ship's dual military and commercial role.

Choosing a target

As with so many other underwater sites, it was chance alone that led to the discovery of the Villefranche wreck. Such was not the case with the *Vasa*, which was 'targeted' by the Swedish engineer Anders Franzén, who analysed contemporary accounts in the early 1950s, before starting to search under water.

In the early 1960s George Bass set out to free the young science of underwater archaeology from depending on chance finds. His plan was to make a systematic inventory of wrecks south of Turkey and choose the most important for excavation. All types of equipment were tried: side-scan sonar, a towed capsule with an observer on board, high-resolution video cameras, a magnetometer and even a small two-seater submarine, the *Asherah*, designed by the Electric Boat Division of General Dynamics. But in the end Bass decided to put his trust in the most cost-effective tool of all: the eyes of local sponge divers, who had discovered the wrecks at Cape Gelidonya, Yassi Ada and Serçe Liman.

Optical illusions

It is now known that the many ancient wrecks reported around Marseilles reflect not only the importance of trade in the region in antiquity but also, and perhaps above all, the lure of the rocky seabed in the area, which is explored throughout the year by a thriving community of local

Fitted with cameras adapted from aerial photography, the submarine *Asherah* (above) was designed to map an underwater site at great speed.

The successive excavations conducted at Yassi Ada in the 1960s by the American-Turkish team led by George Bass and the Bodrum Museum were a testing ground for a vast range of techniques intended to speed up divers' work, increase precision and minimize the hazards of diving at depth. After a 7th-century Byzantine wreck (left, middle ground) was studied, the 4th-century wreck, which lay on a slope going down to a depth of 42 metres (about 140 feet) of water, was excavated using both standard methods – iron grid over the wreck and an air lift for removing sediment (bottom left) – and techniques specific to the excavation team – the two-seater submarine *Asherah*, an underwater telephone booth with a transparent dome (centre) allowing communication between divers and the submersible decompression chamber held under water by a cable attached to 5 tonnes of ballast (top right).

divers. Elsewhere, on low, sandy coasts with few attractions for divers, far fewer discoveries have been recorded. According to the archaeologist Michel L'Hour, the shorter summer season and smaller number of local divers explain the apparent scarcity of wrecks found in Brittany.

In California, where North American sports diving grew up, an exceptionally large community of divers led to the discovery of mortars and other stone objects not easily seen under water, dating from the last phase of local prehistory. As to Florida, which is situated on the return route from the Spanish colonies in America, it has, since the 1950s, attracted a handful of amateur divers, who soon became treasure hunters. Wrecks have been discovered there

M any wrecks from the colonial period have been excavated for commercial purposes over the past fifty years in America and the Bermuda Islands. The Bermuda salvor Teddy Tucker has made several important discoveries, including wrought-iron

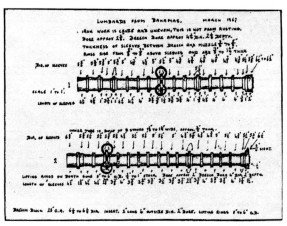

in water 3–6 metres (10–20 feet) deep by swimmers wearing masks, and later excavated by successive waves of divers using a crowbar, an air lift or a water jet.

The Gulf Stream

The object of the explorations pioneered by the professional diver Arthur MacKee, the building contractor Kip Wagner and the diving equipment salesman Melvin Fisher was to hunt for precious objects. But over the years these divers acquired a specific expertise, where the

cannons (above left) from a 16th-century wreck in the Bahamas and a gold pectoral cross set with emeralds from Colombia, found in a late 16th-century wreck in the Bermudas. The first scientific underwater excavations were only carried out in the United States in the 1970s. Above: an excavator with jewelry from the Spanish galleon *Conde de Tolosa*.

Spanish olive jar played the role of the amphora familiar to the divers of the Mediterranean.

Originally Andalusian, the Spanish jar, mostly small and without handles, followed colonial trade as it spread around the world. Its wide distribution – in places as far as Patagonia and Canada, the Philippines and Kenya – reflects the historical importance of Andalusia – specifically Seville and then Cadiz – as a trading post in the days of colonial navigation, from the 16th to the early 19th centuries. But confusion can arise under water: often made of the same material as the amphorae from the same region

– ancient Baetica – and for the same purpose, which was originally to carry olive oil, the Spanish jars found in the Mediterranean have often been mistaken for a particular type of ancient amphora.

While George Bass and his team found the amphora itself one of the major tools for detecting ancient wrecks in Turkey, wreck hunters in Florida have, since the early 1960s, developed an expertise with underwater electronic detection techniques. Wooden wrecks are located by pinpointing solid iron objects used in their construction or carried by them: anchors, cannons, nails, bolts or rigging.

Unlike the amphora, which has been studied for a century by archaeologists interested in antiquity, the Spanish jar was for a long time overlooked. The number of jars in a well-dated context increased dramatically with the discovery of wrecks from the colonial period. Those above were found on the wreck of the *Conde de Tolosa*, which sank in 1724.

In 1724 two Spanish merchant vessels, the *Nuestra Señora de Guadalupe* and the *Conde de Tolosa*, sank on their way from Spain to Veracruz via Havana, off Samana Bay on the island of Santo Domingo. They were carrying luxury goods (top and bottom left) destined for the Creole market in the Americas. The cargo from the *Tolosa* was recovered in 1977 by the American firm Caribe Salvage. The two vessels, recently re-examined by naval archaeologists, are of particular interest because of their role as carriers of mercury (shown centre left, on the *Tolosa*). This very heavy liquid material had forced shipbuilders of the time to reinforce the hold of ships. Mercury, which came from the mines of Almadén in Spain, played a vital part in the extraction of gold and silver in the New World.

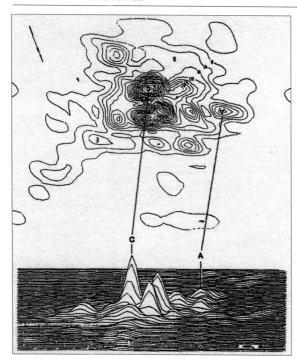

The magnetometer has a variety of uses in archaeology. In large-scale underwater surveys it is towed behind a boat to locate a submerged site (blue diagram opposite). Below: nuclear resonance magnetometers used in 1980 to search for the *Méduse*. In 'intensive' surveys

the magnetometer is used to chart the remains, point by point, even when these are completely buried. Indeed, experience has proved that, within a certain level of intensity – 5 gammas – most of the artefacts existing on the site, including non-metallic objects, are marked out within the magnetic anomaly. The chart above left shows the difference in magnetic field intensity on a 16th-century Spanish wreck site off the coast of Texas.

The magnetic chessboard

The instrument used in the process, the magnetometer, was developed in the utmost secrecy during the Second World War in order to locate German submarines. The magnetometer is sensitive to every local and abnormal variation in the magnetic field. Its remarkable effectiveness in spotting wrecks from the colonial period was demonstrated by the Texan archaeologist J. Barto Arnold III in the experiment he conducted in the 1970s on a mid-16th century Spanish wreck that had foundered on the shores of Padre Island in Texas. As the statistics of scattered remains indicate in this case, the magnetometer allows most of the areas containing debris from a wreck to be circumscribed.

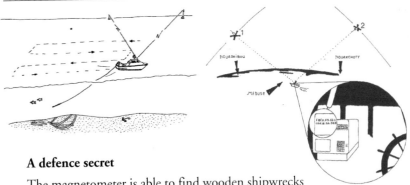

A defence secret

The magnetometer is able to find wooden shipwrecks by detecting iron objects such as nails, ironwork or artillery.

The exceptional sensitivity of the nuclear resonance magnetometer, developed in Grenoble for military and civil use by a department of the French Atomic Energy Commission, made it possible to detect the wreck of the *Méduse* from a distance of nearly a hundred metres (over 300 feet). This French frigate, lost in 1816 in the shallows of the Banc d'Arguin

Inspired by an experience of the Texas Antiquities Committee in looking for a 17th-century wreck off the Mississippi, the search for the *Méduse* combined precise positioning (above, right and left, double frequency Transit satellite receiver and Trident telemetry – the use of radio waves for measuring distances) with magnetic detection of nearly 50 tonnes of ferrous metal on the wreck. Among the hundred or so objects retrieved from the site was a bronze swivel-gun (below left) bearing the mark '85 K' (the cannon's weight in kg), following the recent introduction at the time of the metric system in the French navy. The system was made legal in France in 1801 and was compulsory from 1840.

50 km (30 miles) off the shores of Mauritania, contained 50 tonnes of iron in various forms, including cannons.

Where wrecks are not completely buried in very deep water, the magnetometer is replaced by a side-scan sonar, a kind of underwater 'radar' with a horizontal sweep that can cover large areas of the seabed to show every projection, rock or wreck as a 'shadow' visible on the recording paper or the instrument's screen. In the best cases, such as wrecks that have been well-preserved in cold waters, even masts appear on the screen. Using the recent developments of this technique, Robert Ballard's team has produced impressive digital images of two schooners that sank in Lake Ontario in the early 19th century.

The use of fibre optic and digital signals have made it possible to extend side-scan sonar to any oceanic depth, while other instruments, such as

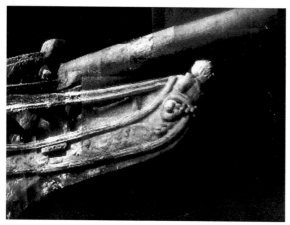

The nature of the sea or lake bottom determines the method used for surveying under water. In 1975 the wrecks of two American warships, the *Hamilton* and the *Scourge*, which had sunk in a squall in 1813, were located by side-scan sonar at the bottom of Lake Ontario. As they were lying at a great depth – 91 metres (300 feet) – where the temperature remained at 4 degrees centigrade, in cold, fresh water, the ships were in excellent condition, with their wood well preserved and their masts still in place. Left: a digital image of the prow of the *Hamilton*, taken from the robot craft *Jason*.

In 1967 it took only a few hours using side-scan sonar to detect a Roman wreck that was lying 90 metres (nearly 300 feet) deep and 24 kilometres (15 miles) north of Yassi Ada in an area of the Turkish coast where a fisherman had, four years earlier, raised a small classical bronze statue in his nets. The pattern of the survey is shown on the left; in the absence of a satellite positioning system, theodolites – surveying instruments – were placed on the neighbouring coast to track the boat's course.

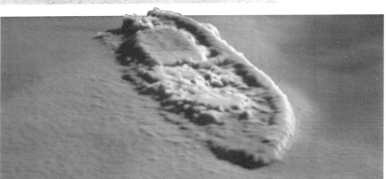

last-generation sub-bottom profilers, inherited from offshore industries or the military, have enabled objects buried beneath the sea floor to be detected. In a feat that would have been unthinkable only ten years ago, it is now possible to 'see' under the mud, with a few centimetres' accuracy, non-magnetic and fully buried objects, such as a tree trunk or the remains of a wooden boat.

Digital images make it possible to assess shapes detected from a distance, such as the American ironclad warship *Monitor* (above, as observed by sonar in 1987), which was sunk in 1862.

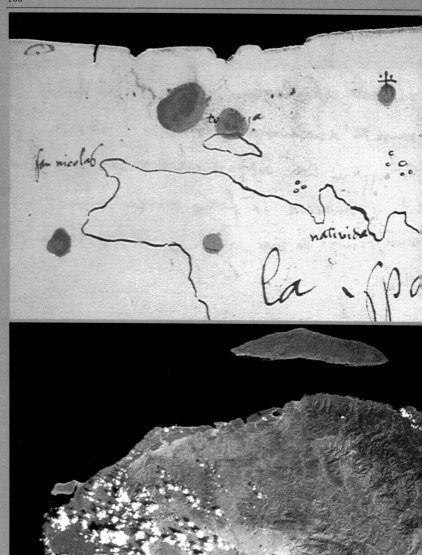

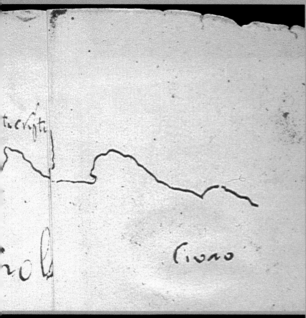

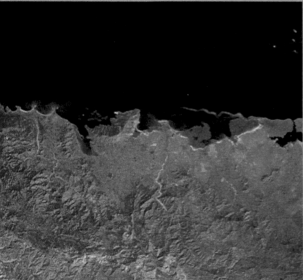

On Christmas Eve 1492 Christopher Columbus' flagship on his first voyage to America, the *Santa María*, foundered on a sandbank on the north coast of Haiti and was destroyed in a few hours by the current, after all hardware had been removed on Columbus' orders. Shortly afterwards Columbus drew a map of the coast (top left), displaying his skills as both a sailor and a cartographer. The outline of this section of the coast has since been greatly altered due to human destruction of forests and alluvial action in estuaries. All that remained of the *Santa María* was the lower hull, making it a difficult archaeological 'target' for those who have searched for it for over fifty years. The clue to the location of the site of the first European ship lost in the New World is a geographical study: the coloured satellite image (bottom left) of the north coast of Haiti today paves the way to a global approach of the archaeological 'landscape'.

The discovery over the past fifty years of more and more underwater sites, some of them in a very good state of conservation, raises the inevitable question: what is to be done with them? Each government has its own answers, but the debate has already reached the great ocean depths.

CHAPTER 7

EXCAVATION, CONSERVATION AND PROTECTION

Recent discoveries have shown that physical and chemical deterioration occurs at all ocean depths. It is evident even at a depth of 3800 metres (over 12,400 feet) on the prow of the *Titanic* in this photograph (opposite) taken in 1991, nearly eighty years after the ship sank. The bronze tweezers on the right, found on the 1st-century BC Roman wreck *Camarat II*, were covered with concretion (right) and X-rayed (far right).

The *Vasa* is rescued in a revolutionary way

The recovery of the *Vasa* in Sweden started with a
highly risky operation. Working head first in the mud
over 30 metres (100 feet) deep, helmet divers from
the Swedish navy dug tunnels underneath the hull,
through which they passed heavy steel wires, in
order to lift the great oak vessel from the seabed.
In successive stages the wreck was slowly brought into
shallower waters at a depth of 17 metres (55 feet).
It was finally raised to the surface in 1961 after
divers had thoroughly reinforced its structure.

After this early 17th-century warship had been
resurrected from the bottom of the sea, many people
with an interest in nautical history held the erroneous
belief that every wreck could now be refloated.
The years to come would show just how unique the
Swedish operation had been. The rescue of the *Vasa*
was an extraordinary technical and financial feat.

When the wreck of Henry VIII's battleship *Mary
Rose* was in its turn refloated in 1982, after over ten
years of difficult excavations, it was clear that the ship
was in a much worse state of conservation than the
Vasa. The British half-ship from the Tudor period
was only raised from the Solent mud thanks to an
almost national effort, volunteered, as in the case of
the *Vasa*, because the *Mary Rose* was a historical
symbol.

The first attempts at conservation

The experience with the *Vasa* focused attention on
an old problem: objects raised from the seabed deter-
iorate rapidly in the open air. In 1840, when artefacts
recovered from the wreck of the *Mary Rose* were sold
at auction, it was remarked that large cannon-balls of
32-lb calibre now weighed only 19 lbs. Thirty years
later the banker Magen and his technicians observed
'bizarre peculiarities' on the cannon-balls from Vigo:
'They break easily and crumble at the least impact,
and seem to be made of countless spokes running
from the centre to the circumference.' In fact, once

SLEIPNER

Opposite: a cannon
ball stripped of
its concretions.

The experience with the *Vasa* was the crowning achievement in a rich Scandinavian tradition of naval archaeology. After several years' work under water the vast wreck was refloated in several stages and finally emerged, supported by two pontoons, after 333 years in the sea, on 24 April 1961 (left). The operation was a great technical feat by the divers and engineers involved. However, at the time the exposure of this mass of oak with a total surface of nearly 14,000 square metres to the air posed a major conservation problem. Furthermore, many wooden remains had come away from the wreck and still lay on the seabed. From 1963 to 1967 divers from the Swedish navy went back to the site, and raised thousands of pieces of woodwork.

exposed to the open air cannon-balls become warm, sweat and are soon reduced to a small mound of oxides.

Wood proved to be even more delicate. In 1850 alum

had been used in Denmark in an effort to stop very old waterlogged wood from decaying. The method was subsequently refined and creosote and linseed oil were applied to the Viking ship found in the Oseberg burial in Norway in 1904. Techniques in the conservation of wood stagnated over the next fifty years. Curiously, polyethelene glycol (PEG), used most frequently in later procedures, had been synthesized by chemists in 1859 but was not made commercially available until 1939, when the American firm Union Carbide marketed it as a softener for all kinds of vegetable fibres as well as for leather and paper, though not at the time for wood.

Unlike the *Vasa*, the *Mary Rose* was thoroughly excavated under water for over ten years. All that remained on the seabed was a half-hull (above), weighing nearly 45 tonnes, that was listing 60 degrees. It was raised in one piece in 1982 and then kept in a purpose-built museum.

The spraying technique developed for the *Vasa* was used in the conservation of the *Mary Rose*, shown undergoing treatment (opposite). A member of the conservation team (left) is inspecting the wood on the ship's stern. The object was to replace the water within the cells of the wood with PEG.

Below: a restored wooden carving, one of seven hundred sculptures found next to the site of the *Vasa*. Most had adorned the outside of the vessel and had either been covered in gold leaf or been painted. They were the work of German and Dutch artists.

Treating wood

Just after the Second World War two teams, one Swedish, the other American, at last suggested that PEG should be used to conserve wet wood so that it did not lose its original shape or break up. In 1956 an article pointed out the significance of polyethelene glycol for archaeology. In the same year Anders Franzén found the *Vasa*. When the wreck was refloated in 1961, a huge bank of material suddenly became available for experiment: 700 cubic metres (24,700 cubic feet) of wood, mostly oak, in need of treatment. The first attempts at conservation showed that, in order to penetrate oak, the PEG needed to be diluted and heated to a temperature of about 65 degrees Celsius. The following method was developed: after seventeen months of treatment each piece of wood was dried for six months. At the end of this period PEG accounted for forty per cent of its weight. It took a couple of decades to treat all the remains.

The interior of the hull of the *Vasa* (left) was full of mud and objects, among which were found the remains of men, women and children who had been allowed on board for her maiden voyage. A total of 24,000 loose artefacts found were treated by being totally immersed in a special chemical bath. The hull presented a very different problem: in addition to years of treatment with chemical spray (twenty-five minutes of spraying with twenty-minute intervals), it was necessary to reinforce the structure by replacing several thousand pieces of iron. The 17th-century divers who had recovered most of the bronze artillery with the help of a diving bell had pierced part of the bridge, which also had to be restored. In 1979, after seventeen years of treating the hull with PEG and preserving agents, the final drying process was started. At the outset the wood contained a very high proportion of water: 1.5 pounds of water for 1 pound of oak, 2 pounds of water for each pound of pine.

The time and the cost of the PEG treatment has driven conservators to look for alternatives, the most promising of which seems to be freeze-drying under atmospheric pressure, started a few years ago by the Canadians. In spite of a partial setback, mainly due to the lack of impregnation with PEG before freeze-drying, the ancient Roman wreck at Marseilles, which was treated all in one block, is an example that augurs well for the future. Directly derived from industrial

The large number of underwater sites discovered has led conservation specialists to invent ways of saving wood and metal from destruction. Since large-scale trials with PEG on the wood of the *Vasa* and freeze-drying on the Roman wreck in Marseilles, intermediate processes were developed. It was found, for example, that although impregnation with PEG was essential for properly conserving wood, deteriorated wood could be stabilized without necessarily saturating it with PEG. Those objects made of a combination of materials (wood and metal or other substances) pose the trickiest problem: they need different, sometimes mutually opposed, treatments. Specialist laboratories now have the skills to treat such objects: the pistol from the wreck of the *Cygne*, sunk in 1808, on the left is shown at various stages of treatment by Archéolyse International – before (top) and after treatment (bottom) and as an X-ray (centre).

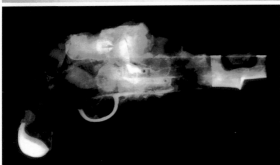

and medical research, freeze-drying involves vaporizing ice without melting it, thus limiting the stresses within the structure of the degraded wood.

The enemy of iron

Metals brought up from the sea into the open air are treated in a variety of ways in order to combat the main threat: salt (sodium chloride), which destroys the structure of the metal by crystallizing as it dries. Conservation techniques, often based on electrolysis, are aimed at eliminating it in a gradual but effective manner. Those wrought-iron anchors retrieved from the sea that are sometimes found exhibited unprotected at ports can very easily give the impression that treatment is not necessary; however, in reality this 'symbolic anchor method' works in only one case out of ten, specifically with heavy wrought iron and in dry climates that experience seasonal rains.

In combining itself with metal, salt forms unstable by-products that threaten the long-term preservation of an object. In crystallizing as it dries, salt also alters the structure of earthenware. Made of lead, brass, cast iron, wood and glazed earthenware, the lavatory raised from the wreck of the warship CSS *Alabama*, which sank off Cherbourg in 1864, epitomizes the composite object that is difficult to treat; it is shown (above) before and after conservation.

'Excavation without conservation is vandalism', according to the Australian Colin Pearson, a pioneer of conservation techniques

In the early 1960s, when diving became a popular sport in Israel, there were nearly thirty thousand practising it in the country. Twenty-five years later two Israeli archaeologists estimated that sixty per cent of the archaeological material under water had already been brought up from the sea, although most of it never reached public collections. In France the underwater archaeologist Luc Long reported that more than ninety-five per cent of the recorded six hundred or so ancient wrecks, ranging from the 6th century BC to the 7th century AD, had been visited and plundered, even at depths of over a hundred metres (over 300 feet).

Industry bears its share of blame for the damage inflicted. In the early 1970s the *Juste*, a mid-18th century warship, was destroyed during dredging to clear the Loire estuary. The few pieces exhibited at the Musée de la Marine in Paris show how well the mud had preserved wood and rigging. Not far from Nantes the intact vessel had been broken to pieces by a dredger, after the failure to engage the public's interest in the same way as had been done for the *Vasa*. Fifteen years later in Holland the archaeologist Thijs Maarleveld and his colleagues, who were all divers, accompanied the dredgers at the port of Rotterdam and proved that rescue archaeology was viable both under water and on land.

The Loire yielded both this mid-18th-century warship, the *Juste*, which was unfortunately destroyed during dredging (above) and a salvaged Bronze Age dugout (below).

People have long made a distinction between archaeology on land and under water. At its most extreme wreck hunting is still proposed as a way of managing the cultural heritage. Actually this fringe industry, which has gripped the collective imagination with discoveries such as the Vigo galleons, is often no more than an exotic branch of the money market aiming to attract investors by luring them with historical information that lies beyond their grasp.

Cultural heritage for sale

The issue is much more complex than it appears. In Vietnam the government entrusted to a commercial salvage business the recovery of a cargo of ancient Chinese porcelain, which was sold at auction in London in 1992. A year later Portugal also succumbed to the temptation of offering for sale part of its underwater heritage before the new legislation was frozen in late 1995. In contrast, some countries such as Greece and Turkey have long pursued and even pioneered wholly different cultural policies. The costly recovery of the Antikythera wreck in 1900 demonstrated the concern felt in Athens for the Greek archaeological heritage. And it was in Turkey sixty years later, thanks to the collaboration of foreign universities, and without dispersing any of its artefacts, that the first major underwater excavations took place and that archaeology was born under the sea.

The British salvage operator Michael Hatcher recovered vast quantities of export porcelain from two wrecks dating from the 17th and 18th centuries in the Far East; 190,000 pieces were sold at auction between 1983 and 1986. The collection above was loaded on to a Dutch East India Company vessel, the *Geldermalsen*, at Canton in 1751 and later sank with the ship.

Deep wrecks and oceanographers

In 1989 France passed very restrictive legislation regarding private ownership of archaeological objects found on its shores. But the government adopted a very different attitude in international waters where French oceanographers were working. When an American firm raised 2600 objects from the *Titanic* on two expeditions in 1987 and 1993, IFREMER (Institut Français de Recherche pour l'Exploration de la Mer) sent its submarine *Nautile* to support the operation. The French action fuelled a controversy and was strenuously opposed by a group headed by the American oceanographer

Robert Ballard who wanted the site to be untouched and left as a shrine.

The recent commercial visits to the luxury liner, which sank on her maiden voyage, have revealed that the wreck suffered a high rate of natural deterioration within the space of a few years; a situation that was

At present only oceanographers and industrialists have the technology to reach great depths (the submarine *Nautile*, above left). Left: treasure from the *Central America*, which sank 2400 metres (7874 feet) in 1857.

again observed by the Russian scientists who went down to the *Titanic* in 1991 in their submarines *Mir I* and *Mir II*, supported by the Russian Academy of Sciences vessel, *Akademik Keldysh*, under the direction of Anatoly Sagalevitch.

A few rust samples taken on this occasion and afterwards analysed in a Canadian laboratory revealed the presence of various bacteria that multiply rapidly,

While the *Titanic* was being filmed, the Russian submarines *Mir I* (above on its deck) and *Mir II* (which took the photograph) explored the wreck, leaving its artefacts in place.

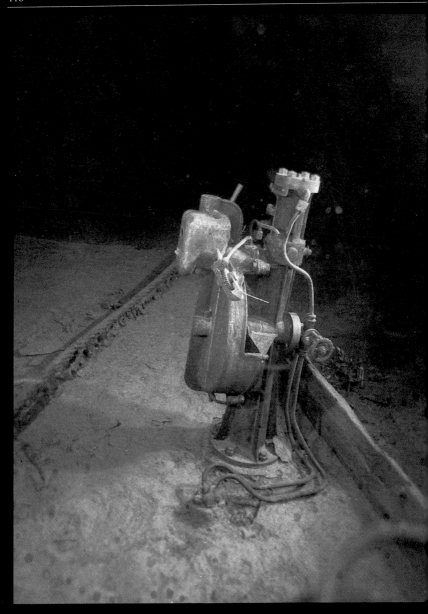

A legendary wreck

The *Titanic* sank on her maiden voyage in 1912 when she hit an iceberg, with great loss of life. In the 1970s the idea of bringing her to the surface was suggested by a novel. A quarter of a century ago experience had suggested to some oceanographers that objects lying at great depths would not be attacked by marine organisms. The widespread shipworm, which destroys wood immersed in sea water, was known, for instance, to be unable to survive at depths of over 200 metres (650 feet). Yet most of the wood on the *Titanic*, which lay at a depth of over 3800 metres (12,468 feet), has been eaten away, showing that other organisms are active at great depths. Recent studies of the *Titanic*, carried out over several years, have produced a better picture of the destructive processes at work – the activity of bacteria in particular.

These and subsequent pages (118–9): photographs of the wreck of the *Titanic* taken by the Russian submarine *Mir II*.

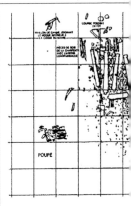

even without oxygen, forming the strange rust-coloured stalactites on the hull.

Australian archaeologists took a pioneering approach when they tackled the engine of one of the first Australian steam coasters, the SS *Xantho*, which had sunk in 1872, by treating and restoring it in the laboratory. This was a turning point in conservation.

A simple but effective remedy against the underwater leprosy of the industrial age has been developed by archaeologists in Australia: the external casing of a car engine made of light alloy is placed on

In the continent of Australia, which was first 'discovered' by Europeans in the 17th century – the north and west coasts by the Dutch mariner Abel Tasman in 1642 and the east by the British explorer Captain James Cook in 1770 – shipwrecks are seen as an important part of the national heritage. Over the past twenty-five years a very active school of underwater archaeology has grown. It is as interested in 17th- and 18th-century Dutch wrecks as in the steam coaster *Xantho*, which was built in Scotland in 1849, and sank on the shores of Australia in 1872. These photographs show its engine being pulled on to the beach (above left) and later (left) being sprayed with caustic soda, while (opposite) work is carried out on the stern.

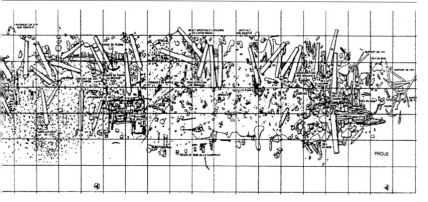

the seabed near the iron or steel remains that are to be conserved. In the same way as zinc anodes protect boat propellers, these cast-offs from the car industry give cathodic protection against the effects of corrosion in salt water.

Wreck sites of the third kind

Suddenly a new concept emerges – underwater objects may be kept *in situ,* so solving the problem of conserving large-scale metallic objects in the open air. The stabilized wreck is converted into a monument, which can be visited by the diving public. Even though many had been pillaged and destroyed in the 1960s and 1970s, when treasure hunters were searching for sunken Spanish galleons, several colonial wrecks near the small coral islands off the Florida coast were made suitable for regular visits by divers. A similar arrangement was carried out in cold water on the untouched wreck of the *Célèbre,* a

What is to be done with our fragile underwater heritage, which is too vast and cumbersome to be excavated or conserved in its entirety? An original solution has been adopted in Quebec. The wreck of the *Célèbre,* a typical French warship, which sank in 1758, was left intact; divers who visit the site are offered the above map, which was made in 1986–7. A different approach was taken with the wreck of a Basque whaling ship, identified as the *San Juan,* which sank in Red Bay, Labrador, in 1565. Because it provided important information on a little-known chapter of Canadian history, the wreck was excavated and its wooden frame dismantled for study in the laboratory.

warship built in Brest in 1755 and sunk during the siege of Louisbourg in Canada in 1758.

The approach adopted by a French research team in the 1970s on an ancient vessel at Madrague de Giens became firmly established. Underwater sites were now to be treated as reservoirs of knowledge, available for each generation to tap in accordance with the techniques and historical questions of the moment.

This approach prevailed even where the entire remains of a wreck had to be removed during an excavation. In Switzerland Béat Arnold made a detailed cast in the laboratory of the dugouts he had retrieved from the lake, and afterwards returned them to the lake that had so successfully protected them from the ravages of time. From 1980 to 1984 a

Linking their research closely with information from archives, the Canadian archaeologists took a very close look at the wooden structure of the 16th-century Basque whaling ship *San Juan*. During its excavation (left) methods previously designed for ancient wrecks in the Mediterranean were used – the wooden structure was dismantled and drawn, piece by piece. A special technique was devised of making moulds of the hull bottom under water. Later a detailed scale model of the wreck was constructed.

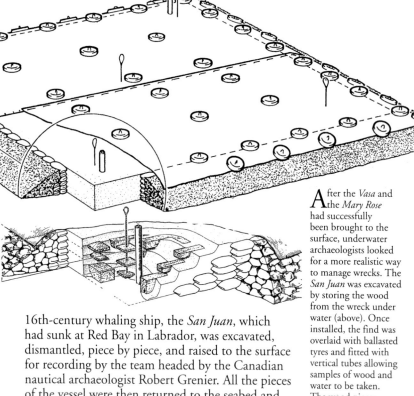

16th-century whaling ship, the *San Juan*, which had sunk at Red Bay in Labrador, was excavated, dismantled, piece by piece, and raised to the surface for recording by the team headed by the Canadian nautical archaeologist Robert Grenier. All the pieces of the vessel were then returned to the seabed and buried under a plastic cover, guaranteed to last several decades.

During the First World War doctors were forced, for want of resources, to select and help those wounded who had the best chances of survival. According to the late Peter Throckmorton, underwater archaeologists face a similar dilemma in that not every site can be studied and preserved.

Robots and deepwater sites

Over the past thirty years scientific and military research has led to numerous archaeological sites

After the *Vasa* and the *Mary Rose* had successfully been brought to the surface, underwater archaeologists looked for a more realistic way to manage wrecks. The *San Juan* was excavated by storing the wood from the wreck under water (above). Once installed, the find was overlaid with ballasted tyres and fitted with vertical tubes allowing samples of wood and water to be taken. The wood pieces, once studied and conserved, thus remained available for later research. At Madrague de Giens (opposite, an Italian krater from the wreck), where a large merchant vessel from the 1st century BC was found, a different course was taken. Part of the keel was removed in order to study the way in which it was assembled with the planking.

being detected at great depths. In 1964 the oceanographic research ship *Amalthée*, based in Nantes, located a Roman wreck at a depth of 400 metres (over 1300 feet) in the Strait of Gibraltar. But it was no more than a mound of amphorae, with no visible remains of the vessel.

A series of experiments conducted by United States oceanographers from the Woods Hole Oceanographic Institution in the North Atlantic since 1971 using the submersible *Alvin* demonstrated that in certain very deep areas, because of reduced bacterial activity, organic material can be preserved to an extraordinary degree: a sandwich left on the seabed was retrieved intact eleven months later.

At that time the American oceanographer Willard Bascom pointed out the potential of deepwater sites between Sicily and Tunisia, dreaming of intact wooden wrecks raised from the bottom of the sea. Yet when, in 1977, the French navy identified the site of

The deepwater submersible *Alvin* (above) carried out various missions – military and oceanographic, including work on the wreck of the *Titanic*.

an ancient wreck off Cap Bénat in France at a depth of 328 metres (over 1000 feet), all that the submarine crew could see was a mound of amphorae some 15 metres (50 feet) long by 6 metres (20 feet) wide. And three years later, when the French submersible *Cyana* came to remove a few amphorae under the direction of the archaeologist Luc Long, no wood was visible.

In 1988 the oceanographer Robert Ballard and a team from the Woods Hole Oceanographic Institution identified ancient remains in the area between Sicily and Tunisia that Bascom had earlier singled out, lying in international waters at a depth of 750–800 metres (about 2500–2600 feet). The following year American oceanographers, this time working with archaeologists, removed 48 sample objects, including 28 amphorae. One of the wrecks, christened *Isis*, proved to be of particular interest as it was one of only fifty wrecks dating from the late 4th century that had been found in the Mediterranean. As in previous cases, the vessel itself was missing. All that was left of it was a few pieces of wood that bore ample witness to the action of marine organisms.

In the early 1970s the American oceanographer Willard Bascom pointed out the archaeological potential of particular areas of the high seas that had been much frequented in antiquity, notably in the Mediterranean. Robert Ballard turned his attention to the region in the late 1980s, resuming the investigation axis indicated by his colleague. The instrument used in the project, a robot craft named *Jason* (below, retrieving an amphora on the *Isis* mission) was operated from the surface. The ROV (remotely operated vehicle) is well suited to the needs of deep underwater archaeological work.

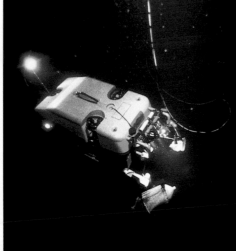

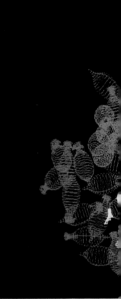

Thanks to ROVs, it is now possible to work under water at great depths without any risk to human life and at reduced cost. Since all archaeologists remain on the surface, the ROV is able to carry out its work uninterrupted for twenty-four hours a day.

Arles IV

The latest major step forward was made by Luc Long and IFREMER technicians carrying out a non-destructive study of a 1st-century AD wreck lying at a depth of 662 metres (over 2000 feet) off the southern coast of France. Christened *Arles IV*, the wreck was

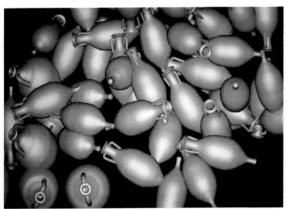

The wreck of the *Arles IV* was photographed (above left) in 1981 by the submersible *Cyana*. It was later examined on archaeological reconnaissance missions in 1989 and in 1993 by the submarine *Nautile*, which was then equipped for stereophotography. This technique involves re-creating three-dimensional forms photographed from the submarine, and was first attempted on an ancient wreck in 1964 in Turkey with the submarine *Asherah*.

In 1993 computer images (left and below left) were used to re-create in three dimensions the mound of amphorae on the *Arles IV* wreck. Among the 950 containers of the first layer of the wreck the archaeologist Luc Long distinguishes three different types of amphorae. The cargo came from the south of Spain (Baetica) in the 1st century AD. After calling at the Balearic Islands, the ship must have headed for the port of Fos at the entrance to the Rhone. Near the wreck Luc Long pointed out '20th-century plastic bottles side by side with garum pots from the time of Caligula'.

located by the submersible *Cyana* in 1981 on a mission 80 km (about 50 miles) off the shores of the Camargue and photographed some years later by the cameras of the oceanographic submarine *Nautile*, using a technique similar to aerial cartography. Freed from the old adage 'every excavation is a destruction', the *Arles IV* experiment paves the way for a 'painless' archaeology where excavation is only one option, a final step. Indeed, international bodies such as UNESCO have now put deep-sea sites on their agenda to establish international standards and protections for the world's historical patrimony.

Every underwater wreck is also a laboratory for non-archaeologists, such as biologists and geologists, providing valuable information on natural history and the evolution of sediment and marine organisms. Sooner or later the question of prohibitive costs of deep-sea missions will be solved when archaeology is included in oceanographic programmes.

Overleaf: discoveries made in the Far East, such as this late 14th–early 15th-century junk found in the Philippines in 1993, are far removed from the European cultural heritage. In the 13th century the explorer Marco Polo marvelled at the great size of the junks on the China Sea and the watertight compartments of the hold that made them unsinkable.

DOCUMENTS

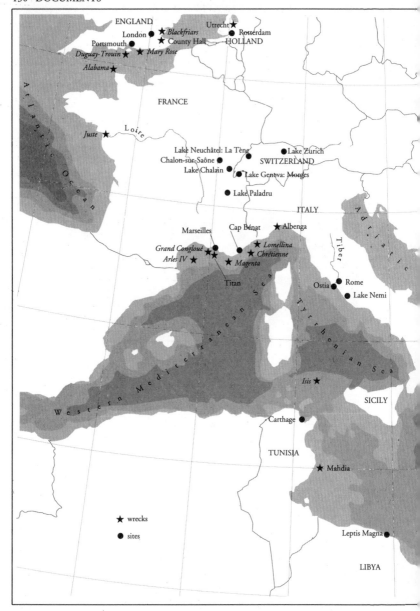

The largest museum in the world

The first great archaeological finds under the sea were made in the Mediterranean, the cradle of western civilization. Europe has been the centre for research into prehistory – it was here that the first underwater excavations of lakes were undertaken in search of the remote human past and here again, above all in the north, that naval archaeology became established from the end of the last century. But such density can be misleading. The number of archaeological sites reported or studied under the Mediterranean reflects a rich past, of course, but it is also indicative of an extensive community of modern divers.

Vast tracts of civilization remain to be explored under water. While Bronze Age vessels were sailing offshore throughout the Mediterranean, history and archaeology remind us that at the same moment, very far away from there, the island people of southeast Asia ventured great distances into the Pacific on craft which had nothing in common with the ancient ships of the Mediterranean.

Jean-Yves Blot
October 1995

Map showing some of the sites mentioned in this book.

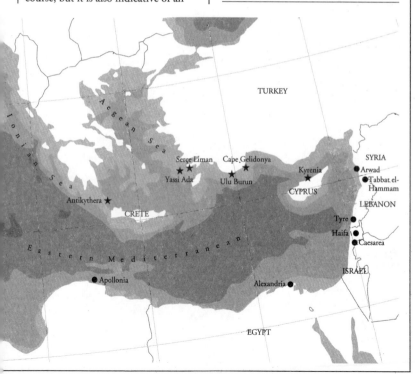

Prehistory

Throughout the ages humans have chosen to live close to water. Tens of thousands of years ago they ventured across vast expanses of open water to reach Australia. Much later, in the Bronze Age, they devised increasingly large and sophisticated wooden craft, which became the vessels of exchanges among the moving frontiers of the known world.

Ice ages and human occupation of the continental shelf

Underwater divers often do not realize they are crossing territories once accessible to prehistoric people, during the coldest part of the last ice age, less than twenty thousand years ago, when the sea level was more than a hundred metres (300 feet) lower than it is now. Nicholas Flemming, geologist, archaeologist and diver, draws his conclusions from the phenomenon.

The archaeological problem
Archaeologists have been aware for several decades that the low sea levels created a larger living space for Stone Age tribes of the Palaeolithic period (older than 10,000 years BC [before present time]), and that migrations between continents and islands were promoted by the creation of land bridges or the narrowing of straits. To show how widely these ideas are accepted I quote from Grahame Clark's *World Prehistory*, published in 1969: 'The radiocarbon dating suggests that

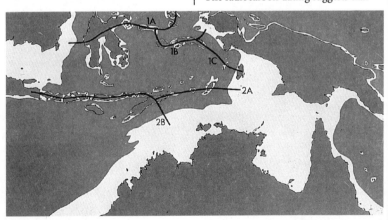

Some 18,000 years ago a large part of the sea north of Australia and in the neighbouring islands was accessible on foot.

the Japanese islands were settled already during the Late Pleistocene, and this after all agrees very well with the fact that at the peak of glaciation (about 20,000 years BP) the main islands were joined to one another and to the mainland of east Asia by way both of Korea and of Sakhalin and the Amur Basin.'

And again: 'The territory of Siberia...owes its interest largely to its position in relation to the New World...through this region the first immigrants must have passed on their way to America, presumably at a time when the land-connection was still intact.'

And again: 'There were periods during the Pleistocene when man could occupy most of Indonesia west of the Wallace line [the evolutionary break between Asia on one side and eastern Indonesia and Australia on the other] without having to traverse open water.... Having once got to Australia by the use of some kind of boats or floats...which at the time of low sea level would have been joined to New Guinea on a broad front by the Sahul Shelf, there was nothing to prevent overland crossing to Tasmania, which was likewise joined to the mainland. The mere fact that sea passages were so narrow during the late glacial period makes it more likely that man first got into Australia at this time.'

So if everybody agrees with this view, what is the problem? Let me quote Clark once again: 'Mesolithic (about 10,000–6000 BP) man could compensate for the reduction in animal grazing ground caused by the spread of forests, and that was by the development of fishing. Much of the evidence for this lies submerged by the rise of the ocean levels due to the continued melting of the ice-sheets.'

In short, all competent archaeologists agree that the continental shelf must have been exploited in a general way for hunting and fishing, and in an explicit way to facilitate continent-to-continent migrations, but we have no direct evidence at all to support this, except that people arrived on the other side! It is implicit that they made the crossing by walking or use of simple craft at times of low sea level, but they could have made the crossing by use of more sophisticated craft over greater extents of water. Everybody agrees that the explanation is obvious, but we do not actually have any proof. This is rather unscientific; in fact, it is the Medieval view of knowledge. As Hilaire Belloc, a turn-of-the-century British humorist, said in his delightfully ironic poem about the microbe: 'Let us never never doubt what nobody is sure about. Scientists, who ought to know, assure us that it must be so.'

So everybody agrees what the answer ought to be, and everybody agrees that all the relevant data are buried beneath the sea. To continue my unscientific quotations, Mark Twain said (in reference to the weather), 'Everybody talks about it, but nobody does anything.'

But a few people have done something, and what they have found provides direct evidence that human beings did live on the continental shelf during the Palaeolithic, Mesolithic, and Neolithic periods, and that the remains of those cultures survived inundation by the oceans.

Nicholas Flemming
'Ice Ages and Human Occupation of the Continental Shelf'
Oceanus, Spring 1985

Charavines and the problem of lake villages

After lake dwellings had been discovered in Europe during the 19th century, people came to believe that villages had been built over water on a foundation of stilts. However, the evidence that emerged in the course of excavations called into question, and sometimes contradicted, this simplistic idea. This was the case with the Neolithic site of Charavines.

For several centuries those who lived and fished near the Swiss lakes had noticed that wooden posts and prehistoric artefacts usually submerged near the bank became exposed in times of drought. In the winter of 1853–4, when the level of all the lakes was lowered dramatically, archaeologists began to take an interest in the subject; Ferdinand Keller [president of the Antiquarian Association of Zurich] was the first to report, at the end of 1854, on the variety of finds and observations made above all at Lake Zurich. Influenced by ethnographic comparisons, this scholar favoured the theory that submerged remains belonged to villages built on platforms over the water, the famous 'lake villages'. Although this explanation was based on the study of only a few sites, it nevertheless won general support; but the reality turned out to be quite different and much more complicated, as the future would reveal.

More than a century of scientific work in Switzerland, Italy, Germany and France has gradually thrown light on these villages: although some details are still being debated, no prehistorian now accepts the theories of the past century. All the archaeological facts, the evidence from excavations, the studies of the evolution of climates and levels of

the lakes have discredited this simplistic idea. We will not consider the general problem of the lake dwellings here, but will look at a few important facts that came from the excavations at Charavines and how they were interpreted.

A village by the edge of the water

People settled by the shore of the lake, on chalk cleared of all vegetation on two separate occasions, and dendroclimatology has shown a slight increase in the dryness of the climate a few years before their arrival. The clay fire-places, which were built directly on to the ground, began to sink as the humidity increased and the ground became softer. The debris of construction (branches, shavings) and daily life (millstones, flint chips and tools, shards, bones, charcoal, seeds) did not lie on floors, which would have been preserved like other wood, had they existed. Parts of the first dwelling that had been destroyed covered the ground – something that would not have occurred had there been any depth of water whatsoever. Livestock wandered round the houses, leaving their droppings on the chalk, which was often damp (as shown by the parasite eggs that have been preserved) but not covered with water. In the very layers of habitat sedimentology has found no lake matter and if seasonal flooding occurred it was of slight duration.

In contrast to other sites in France (the Jura lakes, the lake of Annecy) and Switzerland, the ground must have been permanently dry and firm enough to make it unnecessary to build log 'causeways' as a link, over some tens of metres, between the village and the hinterland.

At Charavines, there is no doubt that the village was built on firm ground very close to the shore and was sometimes

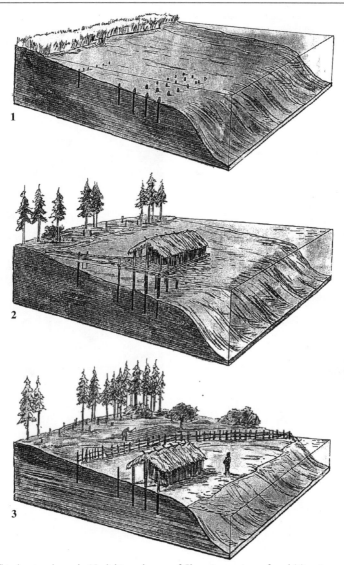

This drawing shows the Neolithic settlement of Charavines: as it was found (1); as it was imagined (2); as it is now known to have been (3).

temporarily affected by the lake overflowing, though daily activities were not unduly disrupted. When the water level rose on a near permanent basis, in the last days of the second village, the people left for good without ever having lived over the water.

Aimé Bocquet
Les Dossiers de l'Archéologie
December 1994

The Bronze Age shipwreck at Cape Gelidonya

In 1960 the young American archaeologist George F. Bass excavated the oldest wreck known at the time, with a European team that included the French aqualung pioneer Frédéric Dumas, who was very interested in classical wrecks. A few years earlier Turkish sponge divers had discovered bronze tools in the waters off southern Turkey at Cape Gelidonya and had showed them to Peter Throckmorton, an anthropologist, diver and journalist. Recognizing the importance of the find, Throckmorton made contact with Bass, who learned how to dive.

The wreck seemed smaller than I had remembered it. Was it possible that those ingots scattered below us were only jetsam, dropped from an overloaded ship trying to clear the cape?

Expedition director George Bass, and Dr Rodney Young, his chief at the University Museum in Philadelphia, had invested the museum's money in this expedition in the belief that here was the wreck of a ship, and that there was a lot more to it than copper ingots and a few bronze tools. No one could be sure until tons of sand and rock were removed. But George, a trained archaeologist and diver, agreed with me that parts of the ship's hull might still exist. If we could find such parts, they might answer

Divers excavating at Cape Gelidonya. The one on the right is using an aqualung.

questions about Bronze Age ships that scholars have posed since the beginning of modern archaeology....

After a few days the wreck began to look like an archaeological site, with meter sticks, tapes and boxes of tools. Different areas soon acquired nicknames. The 'rock' was a boulder [as] big as a truck, dominating the site. The 'platform' was a rock that held a heap of ingots above the sand. The 'gully' ran between the rock and the 'cliff'....

One day Dumas [the most experienced diver on the expedition and a founder of the French navy's underwater research team] noticed that the platform was hollow underneath. He chipped at the overhang and exposed the corner of an ingot. Part of what we had taken for rock was actually copper, welded into a mass by sea-deposited limestone. More chipping showed that half the platform was metal.

While we pondered how to handle this find, Dumas noticed an oddly shaped stone at the gully's mouth and gave it an experimental bash with his hammer. A cloud of green 'smoke' rose – copper sulphate. Dumas had exposed another ingot, under another heap of concreted metal objects.

Although familiar with the limestone growth which covers all objects exposed under water in the Mediterranean, we were not prepared for growth that was eight inches [twenty cm] thick in some spots. We re-examined the gully and found it full of metal. In places ingots were stacked five deep. We went wild with joy, and sent off happy telegrams to our sponsors….

When the concretion was chipped off the ingots, many seemed in as good condition as when they left the foundry more than three millenniums ago. Miss Taylor [of the University of London Institute of Archaeology, a specialist in Bronze Age material] called some typically Cypriote. Others were of a type heretofore found only in Sardinia….

Most of the ingots were the familiar 'oxhide' shape I had seen on my first trip. But we also found others, each resembling a discus; some had been broken into halves, quarters, eighths, or smaller pieces, perhaps as units of exchange….

A lump of rock at the gully's mouth also seemed full of objects. We raised it with great labor, to find only the green stains of decomposed copper.

But our disappointment vanished when we explored the sand underneath the lump and found a row of planks extending into the gully. Sandwiched between the wood and a compacted mass – in this case copper and bronze pieces and unbelievably fragile organic matter – was a layer of ballast stones. It was an undisturbed cross-section of the ship. At last! Now we had visible proof that we were dealing with the remains of a ship, and not with objects thrown overboard.

Peter Throckmorton
'Oldest Known Shipwreck
Yields Bronze Age Cargo'
National Geographic Magazine,
May 1962

The Ulu Burun shipwreck

Twenty-four years after the discovery of the Cape Gelidonya shipwreck, which dated from 1200 BC, George F. Bass began to excavate an even older wreck, which was to throw light on the Bronze Age in the eastern Mediterranean.

I felt no emotion as I scanned the cargo for the first time that summer of 1984. I was standing upright, my diving fins resting on a rock outcrop 150 feet [45 metres] below the surface of the Mediterranean.

The world's oldest known shipwreck lay before me – the shapes of jars and copper ingots dated back to the 14th or early 13th century BC. But I had no more than five minutes to plan its excavation.

Five minutes to estimate the lie of the ship's hull beneath its cover of sand and cargo. Five minutes to decide where to place our air-filled Plexiglas dome – dubbed the 'phone booth' – in which our divers might take refuge in an emergency or telephone the surface.

Five minutes to decide what mapping techniques we would use. Five minutes spent fighting nitrogen narcosis caused by breathing at such depth.

Thousands of dives over more than a quarter of a century had trained me to fight the dullness clouding my mind. But the effort left no room for fancy or romance. Quickly I drew up a mental plan of action and a list of priorities, then started for the surface....

Long experience has taught us that the best sources of information about ancient shipwrecks are the divers on Turkey's sponge boats. For search purposes the divers are far more valuable than the most sophisticated sonar and magnetometers in existence. Cemal [Pulak, assistant excavation director] and Don [Frey, president of the Institute of Nautical Archaeology] recently calculated that in a single four-month summer season the divers on twenty-five boats spend a combined total of about 20,000 hours roaming the seabed in the quest for sponges. The figure works out to the equivalent of about two years' underwater search by one marine archaeologist – without coming up for air!

As a result we have come to know the sponge divers well, and during the winter Don and his Turkish colleagues give slide-show lectures in the divers' villages to teach them what to look for in the way of ancient wrecks....

As we carefully surveyed the site, we found that the ship's principal cargo had been copper ingots. There were about 200 of them – more than six times the number we had found at Cape Gelidonya. Each of the ingots weighs around 60 pounds [27 kg], the equivalent of an ancient talent.

Months later I ran across a passage in one of the tablets from Tell el-Amarna mentioning a promised gift of 200 talents of copper from the king of Alashiya to an Egyptian pharaoh. The coincidence was stunning, and I could only speculate: Was the promised shipment ever sent from Alashiya, which we believe to be Cyprus? Did it reach Egypt? Or is it possible that the gift ended up on the sea floor off the point known today as Ulu Burun?

The chances that we had found that very cargo seemed remote, though I was soon convinced that the Ulu Burun ship nonetheless carried a royal consignment of some sort dating from the 14th century BC – in the Late Bronze Age, a period roughly between 1600 and 1050 BC.... Because of the dangerous depth – 140 to 170 feet [460 to 560 metres] – we limited our initial time on the wreck to only five minutes a dive. We gradually increased the time to twenty minutes twice a day, though it required long periods of subsequent decompression on pure oxygen.

Almost at once the wreck fulfilled our expectations. The first dives yielded disk-shaped copper ingots as well as the familiar four-handled style, a mace head of stone, a Canaanite amphora full of glass beads, and a second amphora filled with orpiment, a yellow sulfide of arsenic once used as a pigment.

We also brought up samples of a grayish, brittle material that later proved to be 99.5 per cent pure tin – the very substance that spurred on the Bronze Age but is seldom found from that period in raw form.

'If these are remnants of tin ingots, they're the oldest ever found,' I told the staff over dinner one night. 'If we could match such ingots chemically with tin from a known source, we could solve one of the great mysteries of the Bronze Age.'

Soon afterward we did find tin ingots. A day or two later, Tufan [Turanli] brought up what appeared to be a bronze dagger, though the concretion surrounding it disguised all but the general shape. The story of the dagger demonstrates that many of our most exciting discoveries often are made not on the sea floor but in libraries, museums and laboratories long after our expeditions end.

The dagger was so encrusted that I had no idea of its date or origin. We stored it wet until the season ended, and then conservator Jane Pannell cleaned and preserved it at our laboratory in Bodrum....

If one multiplies the story of the dagger by 1224 – the number of artefacts we have so far raised and catalogued from the wreck at Ulu Burun – one begins to understand what underwater archaeology is really all about. On...average we devote two years to conservation and research for every month of diving on site. In short, nautical archaeologists spend comparatively little time in wet suits!...

Even I would never have imagined a site with such an abundance of new information for scholars from so many fields – Egyptologists, geographers, Homeric scholars, students of ancient metallurgy, glass, construction, sea trade, agriculture, art and religion.

In short, we are salvaging the greatest of all treasures – the treasure of knowledge.

George F. Bass
'Oldest Known Shipwreck Reveals Splendors of the Bronze Age'
National Geographic Magazine
December 1987

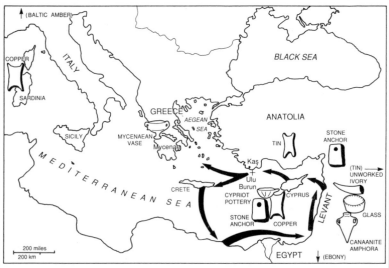

A map showing the probable route taken by the Ulu Burun ship and the likely sources from which the materials for the various artefacts came.

An insight into Bronze Age trade

It is difficult for the archaeologist to learn what commodity was traded against what other commodity, and to understand the mechanics of trade. The discovery of the shipwreck of a trading vessel, complete with cargo, is thus of particular value. In 1982, just such a wreck, dating from the 14th century BC, was found at Ulu Burun, near Kas, off the south Turkish coast in 43 metres (141 feet) to 60 metres (198 feet) of water. It was excavated between 1984 and 1994 by George F. Bass and Cemal Pulak of the Institute of Nautical Archaeology in Texas.

The ship's cargo contained about 10 tons of copper in the form of 354 of the so-called 'oxhide' ingots (i.e. shaped like an oxhide) already known from wall paintings in Egypt and from finds in Crete, Cyprus, and elsewhere. The copper for these ingots was almost certainly mined on the island of Cyprus (as suggested by lead-isotope analysis, and trace-element analysis). Also of particular importance are nearly a ton of ingots and other objects of tin found on the sea floor in the remains of the cargo. The source of the tin used in the Mediterranean at this time is not yet clear. It seems evident that at the time of the shipwreck, the vessel was sailing westwards from the east Mediterranean coast, and taking with it tin, from some eastern source, as well as copper from Cyprus.

The pottery included jars of the type known as Canaanite amphorae, because they were made in Palestine or Syria (the land of Canaan). Most held turpentine-like resin from the terebinth tree, but several contained olives, another glass beads, and another an arsenical compound called orpiment. Similar jars have been found in Greece, Egypt, and especially along the Levantine coast.

The exotic goods in the wreck included lengths of a wood resembling ebony, which grew in Africa south of Egypt. Then there were Baltic amber beads, which came originally from northern Europe (and which probably reached the Mediterranean overland). There was also ivory in the form of elephant and hippopotamus tusks, possibly from the Mediterranean, and ostrich eggshells that probably came from North Africa or Syria. Bronze tools and weapons from the wreck show a mixture of types that include Egyptian, Levantine, and Mycenaean forms. Among other important finds were several cylinder seals of Assyrian, Kassite, and Syrian types, ingots of glass (at that time a special and costly material) and a chalice of gold.

This staggering treasure from the sea bed gives a glimpse into Bronze Age trade in the Mediterranean. George Bass considers it likely that the trader started his final voyage on the Levantine coast. His usual circuit probably involved sailing across to Cyprus, then along the Turkish coast, past Kas and west to Crete, and perhaps northwest to the Mycenaean sites of Greece or even further north, as hinted by the discovery on the wreck of spears and a ceremonial sceptre/mace from the Danube region of the Black Sea. Then, profiting from seasonal winds, he would head south across the open sea to the coast of North Africa, east to the mouth of the Nile and Egypt, and, finally, home again to Phoenicia. On this occasion, however, he lost his ship, his cargo, and probably his life at Ulu Burun.

Colin Renfrew and Paul Bahn
Archaeology:
Theories, Methods and Practice, 1996

Excavating ancient ships

The complexity of ancient wooden shipbuilding presented a challenge to the first excavators. Faced with an increasing number of underwater finds, archaeologists gradually developed new tools adapted to this specific context and made use of new technology to explore these early wrecks.

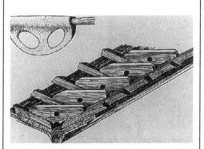

Reconstruction of the lower part of the hull at Grand Congloué.

Grand Congloué: one or two ships?

Lying at the approach to Marseilles, a large trading port that dates back to antiquity, the rocky island of Grand Congloué has been a dangerous area for ships throughout the ages. In 1952 it was chosen, unfortunately in the event, as the site of a major exercise in underwater archaeology. Because of their crude methods of analysis, the excavators failed to recognize that they were investigating not one ancient wreck but two, one on top of the other.

The first Greco-Italic amphorae and Italic amphorae bearing the name of [the potter] Sestius from the Grand Congloué wreck were brought up in the nets of fishermen from La Ciotat in 1936. The site, which lay at a depth of between 32 and 45 metres [105 and 148 feet] in a belt of treacherous islands east of Marseilles, was excavated on and off between 1952 and 1957 by a team headed by Commandant Jacques-Yves Cousteau, in close association with the then Director of Antiquities, Fernand Benoît. Non-diving archaeologists worked closely with either professional or amateur divers who had little knowledge of excavation methods in the first large-scale operation of underwater archaeology. It introduced methods that were later to be adopted as standard in many similar projects. The *Calypso*, which was moored above the site, served as a floating base and maintained the air supply of a powerful air lift that the aqualung divers used to clear the wreck site.

The long excavations were temporarily halted in 1957 and later resumed by Yves Girault in 1961. That year Benoît published the main findings in the fourteenth supplement of *Gallia* under the title 'L'épave du Grand

Amphorae being raised from the wreck of the *Calypso*.

Congloué à Marseille'.... Even before this report appeared, questions had been raised about the conflicting dates of materials found on the same wreck. The presence of several hundred Dressel form 1 amphorae and of a cargo of Campanian ceramics, Greek and Greco-Italic amphorae thought to be older, supported the theory that one wreck lay on top of another....

The apparent intransigence Benoît showed in his article – he did not consider that more than one wreck might be involved – stood in striking contrast to the observations he had made in his excavation diary some years earlier....

The diary clearly reveals that problems frequently arose in the excavation and interpretation of the cargo. The contradictions that went unmentioned in the 1961 publication seem to us to point strikingly to the existence of two wrecks. There is almost daily evidence of disagreements between divers, of Benoît's uncertainties, and of the confusion produced on studying the site.

It was also apparent throughout the excavation and in much of the site that the two groups of materials from different periods in history were clearly separated by wooden remains. Although these pieces of the wooden structure were for a long time taken to be the deck of one and the same ship, the many sketches in the excavation diary strongly indicate that they in fact belonged to the bottom of the hull.

Extracts from the excavation diary

16 August 1952: We are dealing with a ship on the north side of Grand Congloué, whose cargo is spread along the slope between 28 and 44 metres [92 and 144 feet]: crockery at the top – near the bottom, two types of amphorae with long necks, vertical lips and rounded bellies. The crockery is of the type common in the oppida of Provence from the 4th to 2nd centuries.

22 August 1952: The ship forms a mound, with amphorae on one side, and on the other amphorae alternating with piles of crockery.... Large superposed pieces of rock from the cliff, to be removed.... The first baskets containing the top layer are raised: new shapes, fish dish...twenty different types.

End August 1952 (extracts from Fréderic Dumas): Each time we dive, the wreck looks bigger, so one evening Jacques [Cousteau] and I measured it with a string: 20 by 8 metres [66 by 26 feet]. But how far does it go under the sand? Swapping impressions, the divers speak of a rock weighing some ten tonnes. Jacques saw amphorae higher up on the slope, I saw some lower down; rock has tumbled on to the wreck.... August is drawing to a close.... We are removing things from this huge ship without knowing the basic rules of archaeology. While gathering these objects, we do not break into the wreck, so we have not to make a special effort to create a hole and reach wood from the hull to know where we are....

25 September 1952: Two large blocks lying on the amphorae are put to one side...the lower layer seems to consist only of spinning-top amphorae: did the ship call into north Italy and take on a second cargo of SES[TIUS] amphorae, as the crockery is from Campania?...

13–8 October 1952: The lower layers of amphorae are uncovered with the air lift.

19 October 1952: It appears that the upper layer consists of Roman amphorae and the lower of 'spinning-tops'. The dredge cuts in at right angles to the axis of the ship....

26 October 1952: The part of the wreck lying southwest is cleared with an air lift. Commandant and Dumas raise pieces of

lead sheathing studded with copper.... Many pieces of wood are brought up by the air lift, some pegged with reinforced treenails.

29 October 1952: Lead sheathing, wood, probably from the ship's deck....

1 March 1953 (extract from Frédéric Dumas): Near the cliff Bébert shows me ends of blackish frames eaten away by shipworm; he has spotted the keel.

4 March 1953: Contact with Port Calypso: Campanian dishes, new shapes.

5 March 1953: Under what we took for the keel, a layer of amphorae: two wrecks or one wreck folded back on itself? The question becomes more complicated.

6 March 1953: Phone call to Lallemand: confirmation.

13 March 1953: The last observations over (or under) the boat: the keel (oak) has been devoured by lithophagous molluscs; all that remains is an incrustation in the sand. Preserved parts of the frame – the lead sheathing on the rock gives the outline of the stern (?). A cargo of straight Italic amphorae, and Greek amphorae above and a few Campanian dishes with their glaze preserved. A cup with a bell-shaped rim...with red circle and four palm leaves....

27 April 1953: The perspective of the ship seems to show that it has one deck with a cargo of amphorae above the hold, and pottery and sailors' accommodation below. The wood with the square section seen earlier belonged to the deck and not the keel.

28 April 1953: Superposed decks – two or three Italic tiers – deck (large pieces with caulking and lead), Greek amph[orae] and Campanian crockery – the planking would have had an oak frame – lead.

6 May 1953: The supposed bottom of the ship would be the between-decks and it is assumed that there are two wrecks, one on top of the other, the amphorae of Sestius occupying the south part against the rock, without Greek amphorae and crockery interposing, the latter being below. This could be explained by the different locations of the cargoes.

11 May 1953: Telephone call. Agreed that the ship's two between-decks are very close together – conclusion: a single wreck.

Luc Long
'Les épaves du Grand Congloué, étude du journal de fouille de Fernand Benoît' *Archéonautica*, 1987

The Roman wreck found at Cap Bénat in France at a depth of 328 metres (1077 feet)

Since the Second World War, the offshore oil industry and the military have developed a series of small submarines. The resulting discoveries made it possible to consider wrecks at great depths as a part of our heritage, within reach of modern investigation.

As the use of a submersible and its back-up services costs between 50,000 and 250,000 French francs [£7000 and £35,000 or $10,000 and $50,000] a day, depending on the individual circumstances, an archaeologist will not lightly turn down an invitation to visit a deepsea wreck for free. Although somewhat rare, such opportunities, offered by military, public or private bodies, lead in most cases to a short, specific isolated operation.

The Cap Bénat IV wreck was studied in such circumstances. Discovered in 1977 by the French Navy submersible the *Griffon*, several nautical miles east of Toulon at a depth of 328 metres [1077 feet], the site consisted of a mound of Italian wine amphorae in the 'old' Dressel form 1 A, which led the shipwreck to be dated to 130–110 BC.

The first scientific investigation was made the same year by an archaeologist from the French underwater research team DRASM, who accompanied the navy on the *Griffon*. In 1980 DRASM examined the site again, this time on a

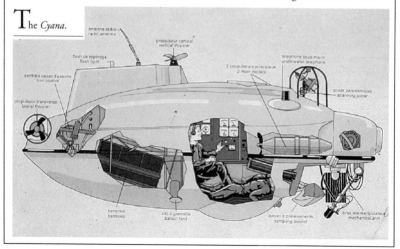

The *Cyana*.

antenne radio – radio antenna
propulseur vertical – vertical thruster
flash de repérage – flash light
centrale caisse d'assiette – trim control
propulseur transversal – lateral thruster
telephone sous-marin – underwater telephone
2 propulseurs principaux – 2 main motors
sonar panoramique – scanning sonar
batteries – batteries
silo à grenaille – ballast tank
panier à prélèvements – sampling basket
bras télémanipulateur – mechanical arm

trial dive by the submersible *Cyana* at the invitation of CNEXO (now IFREMER, the Institut Français de Recherche pour l'Exploration de la Mer). Together the two operations, which each lasted a few hours, allowed the dimensions of the site to be roughly assessed and photographs and video recordings to be taken.

The amphorae, which had few concretions on them, formed an oval measuring 15 metres [49 feet] long by 5 or 6 metres [16 or 20 feet] wide. Towards the centre of the pile the containers, which were closely overlapping one another, clearly showed that two layers were superposed. The average concentration of amphorae, all layers considered, was five per square metre [square yard]. On the peripheries of the site, the amphorae had overturned and lay chaotically on their sides; this must have occurred when the wooden sides of the ship, having gradually swollen with water, gave way under the load. Taking into account the size of the site and the concentration of containers in the centre of the pile, the cargo is reckoned to consist of between 300 and 350 units in total.

The possible existence of a third layer, buried in the sediment, would probably bring the total to more than 500. Experts also located several urn-goblets stacked and making the stem section of the ship materialize....

On each of the two dives, performed at different times, a number of amphorae – fourteen in all – were removed by the remote-controlled arm of the submersibles. These were a precise sample of the containers and allowed them to be checked for stamps or other marks. Each amphora was deposited in a geologist's net that had, with some difficulty, been dragged close to the wreck by the base ship, the *Noroit*....

The presence on the amphorae of a superb white polyp, *callogorgia verticillata*, never previously reported in the area was of interest to biologists.

Luc Long
'100 sites historiques d'intérêt commun méditerranéen'
Protection du Patrimoine archéologique sous-marin en méditerranéen, 1995

The evolution of shipbuilding techniques

J.-C. Négrel and his diving colleagues noticed a distinct but subtle evolution in shipbuilding techniques on a 4th-century wreck excavated off the French Mediterranean coast. The lead sheathing of the hull, which was still frequently used until the end of the 2nd century, had disappeared, but it was above all the internal construction of the ship that drew the attention of the diver-archaeologist. Metal bolts held the pieces of the frame together.

[The keelson] is solidly attached to the floor timbers and the keel by an iron bolt with a washer covered in cast lead....

In [the wreck in] Monaco the bolt was made of copper, while on the 4th-century Roman vessel at Yassi Ada it was made of iron. This strong link between the keel, frame and keelsons recurs at three points on the La Luque wreck, a characteristic that is increasingly to be found on more recent ships. A technical evolution seems to have taken place: the role of the planking in the whole structure decreases in favour of the frame. The planking becomes thinner, the mortise and tenon joints remain but the internal skeleton of the ship plays a more important role thanks to the links that exist between the keel, the frame and the keelsons. These ribs are no longer only simple reinforcements but begin to contribute actively to the whole structure. The lead sheathing is eliminated and iron fastenings, more resistant, introduced, and in the 7th-century Byzantine ship at Yassi Ada the hull owes its strength more to the skeletal framework than to its planking, which still features tenons and mortises.

J.-C. Négrel
'Une coque du Bas-Empire dans la rade de Marseille'
Archeologia, February 1973

Keep it simple, stupid (KISS)

Nick Rule, an English survey consultant who has written various programmes for use in mapping underwater sites, explains why he defends the principle of KISS (Keep it simple, stupid) and what problems divers face in working under water.

Time/physiological effects

It is well known that divers can spend less time in deep water sites than in shallow water sites for fear of 'the bends' (decompression sickness). For example, divers on the *Mary Rose*, at an average depth of 12 metres [40 feet], rarely totalled more than three hours per day under water and averaged much less. This does not compare favourably with land archaeology and is a major factor in the cost of underwater excavations, which is often measured in dollars per hour of 'bottom time'.

Psychological effects

Although I am yet to find conclusive published research, I am convinced that as soon as I submerge my intelligence significantly drops. This idea is enshrined in the well-known 'Martini law', which states that every 10 metres [32 feet] of depth has the same effect as drinking a double Martini.

Corrosion

The sea is a harsh environment, where sensitive equipment can easily get dropped or otherwise broken, where one grain of sand in a seal can cause a leak, and where almost everything corrodes rapidly. In short, any technique to be used for underwater mapping must use extremely robust equipment. It is not purely for financial reasons that the tape measure is the preferred tool of many underwater archaeologists.

Impact of the above upon accuracy

A professional diver has been jokingly defined as someone who, when put naked into a padded cell and given two ball bearings, will rapidly manage to break one and lose the other. Given the real life problems described above, it is not difficult to see how the joke has arisen and how it applies to all underwater workers. The important thing is that all of the above problems contribute to a high error rate under water. I have studied the rate of blunders recorded during the mapping of various sites (blunders are here defined…as non-systematic errors)….

In a database of 3731 tape measurements (maximum value 43.41 metres, average value 6.58 metres) from 12 surveys on 11 sites, 151 measurements (4 per cent) were rejected as blunders whilst drawing up the plans…. It is no wonder that such plots for large sites can take weeks or months.

Nick Rule
'Some Techniques for Cost-effective Three-dimensional Mapping of Underwater Sites'
Computer Applications and Quantitative Methods in Archaeology
1995

New technique speeds up excavation

At Yassi Ada, a rocky islet off the Turkish coast, George F. Bass and his team tackled a 7th-century wreck, in which the wood of the hull had been partly preserved, thereby adding to the recording work for the divers.

Our wreck lay with its deepest point in 120 feet [36 metres] of water – 30 feet [9 metres] deeper than our Bronze Age ship. Therefore we had to dive nearly to the limit at which aqualung archaeologists can work efficiently.

Using information from Navy diving tables, we set 43 minutes a day – in two separate dives with a three- to six-hour pause between – as the maximum time we could stay at this depth. And so four divers could do no more than three man hours of work each day. Hovering over wire grids, we would sketch the objects beneath us on sheets of frosted plastic, using graphite crayons. But eventually we devised a better mapping method, and for two weeks nearly fifteen divers concentrated on building our most advanced and most useful device.

First we placed a scaffolding of pipe and angle iron over the entire wreck. To accommodate…the slope of the site, we arranged the scaffolding in nine giant steps. Then we constructed two movable towers, each 13 feet [4 metres] high, to hold our cameras in a fixed focus. Thus we could take grid photographs quickly at each step of the scaffolding. We could plot planks and nail holes exactly to the centimeter. The time-consuming business of drawing under water was practically eliminated, and underwater archaeology had moved another stride forward.

George F. Bass
'Underwater Archaeology'
National Geographic Magazine
July 1963

An archaeologist excavating the Byzantine wreck at Yassi Ada.

Excavating a late-Roman shipwreck using the ROV *Jason*

The choice of site

In the spring of 1988 two sites were identified by Robert Ballard, one for archaeological, the other for geological investigation. They were identified by means of a towed survey system named *Argo* using a digital Electronic Still Camera (ESC) and black-and-white video SIT cameras…. The archaeological site was located in international waters off the NW tip of Sicily. It was identified on the basis of scattered ancient amphorae documenting an ancient trade route and the remains of a separate ancient shipwreck nicknamed *Isis* for the benefit of television programs for children….

Program of work

The archaeological portion of the project lasted from 6 to 20 May. The first week was devoted to live television broadcasts, the second week to survey work. Two archaeological areas were surveyed, mapped and photographed by ROV *Jason* and the towed support vehicle *Medea*. Three high-sensitivity color video cameras (one of broadcast quality) and a 35-mm still camera were mounted on *Jason* with 2000 watts of incandescent lighting. *Medea* also carried 2000 watts of incandescent lighting. Black-and-white footage was shot from the towed support vehicle with a Silicon Intensified Target (SIT) video camera. No digging or imaging beneath the surface took place in 1989. Due to technical constraints, the project was limited to an imaging survey and the recovery of selected archaeological material for identification and study. Photographic coverage included a total of about eighty-four hours of color video.

The two sites and their underwater environment

One site, which we call the trade route north of Skerki Bank, covered an area of c. 6 km E–W by c. 5 km N–S. Some seventy amphorae are scattered over this area, they lie roughly in a line running NW–SE and appear to relate to an ancient trade route in use at least from the Roman republic to early medieval times. Within this area six possible sites of wrecks were identified using the criterion of three or more amphorae of the same type or similar date found together. In this area ROV *Jason*, moving at 0.5 knots, searched in a grid pattern. It could cover an area of about 500 meters E–W by 250 meters N–S in five hours, on lines spaced 25 meters

apart. This new technology is thus able to search wide areas of the sea floor effectively. Comprehensive study of trade routes and patterns of commerce in this area are now possible....

The other site...was a wreck, named the *Isis*, located c. 1.5 km SE of the southernmost cluster of amphorae of the first area. A group of largely complete amphorae and other archaeological material was documented. The visible surface material from this wreck covered about 10 square meters. The main concentration fell in an area 5 x 6 meters [16 x 20 feet] and lay on a line running NE–SW, with the artefacts appearing at the N end. Its depth varied from 740 meters [2430 feet] at its S end to 800 meters [2625 feet] towards the N end. The central part of the wreck was mapped and photographed by ROV *Jason* as it worked precisely across the 10 square meters. Forty-eight artefacts were documented and ten mostly complete amphorae and five complete common wares were chosen for lifting, as well as a lamp, the upper part of a cylindrical millstone, sections of iron anchors and wooden planking.... Various marine animals were observed on the site, including crabs, shrimps, eels and groupers. Shrimp often filled the video screens, apparently attracted by the ROV's lights to the sea bottom... These marine forms are common in the upper zones but their presence at these depths in the abyssal zone is of interest. Each amphora had its own unique ecology revealed through the different organisms that lived upon it. The amphorae therefore provide a unique collection for a study of deep-sea environments.

Anna Marguerite McCann
'The Late-Roman Shipwreck
Northeast of Skerki Bank'
Journal of Roman Archaeology, 1994

The modern era

Since the Renaissance the oceans crossed by ships have taken on the character of a worldwide network. The archaeology of the period reflects this great movement of ships: each artefact found on a site is liable to have come from far away, sometimes the opposite end of the world to the place where it was lost or damaged. Historical research and archaeology for this post-medieval world overlap more and more closely as documentary sources become increasingly available.

Why hunt for the *Mary Rose*?

The British historian, diver and writer Alexander McKee did not call himself an archaeologist. Yet his reasons for setting out in quest of the Mary Rose *clearly define the aims and framework of an archaeological inquiry.*

Even in the local sub-aqua club I was regarded as something of an impractical visionary. I was given to rhapsodizing on the potential of the Solent area, stressing its importance as a focal point for shipping of some sort for at least 5000 years. Many vessels, I argued, must have been wrecked and buried in the preserving mud to lie there forgotten, including the ship whose name had preoccupied me for so long. The proposition I put to Towse and Baldry in January 1965 was that we should organize a search aimed specifically at the *Mary Rose*, the most important of the known, named wrecks in our area, but also, I explained, the most important known wreck in northwest Europe.

For nautical historians there was at that time a great gap in their knowledge, stretching from the end of the well-documented Viking period in about 1100 AD to the beginning of the 18th century. From that date to Nelson's time, the British National Maritime Museum alone boasted no less than 25,000 ship plans, plus many ship-builders' models. Almost the only facts missing from the record were the colours of the carpets in the captains' cabins. Wrecks of this later period, although old, were not worth looking for.

The *Mary Rose*, however, was a different proposition. There were no plans of her or of any similar ship, nor were there shipbuilders' models. And yet she had been the first English battleship to have gunports and to mount

Pages from Alexander McKee's excavation notebook on the *Mary Rose*, 21 October 1969.

complete batteries of heavy siege artillery – a really key ship in the development process at a time of rapid technological change. Virtually nothing was known about her; there was only a single authentic picture and that not very informative. The hull alone would be a priceless store of information, but there were also the guns, many of them of unknown type, again from a time of rapid technological change. And there was the crew – at least 400 men and possibly as many as 700 – of whom I was certain several hundred must remain in and around the wreck. Many would be complete with their clothes, equipment, weapons, personal possessions and so on: a complete cross-section of Tudor military and naval society – aristocrats and commoners, bowmen and mariners, pikemen and gunners, officers and men – all cut down in the same place on the same day, in their prime. Unlike the contents of a cemetery, where the old and the sick are laid in their winding sheets, a thorough scientific examination could almost bring these men of the *Mary Rose* back to life, so great would be the detail and so representative the remains. No land site could offer such a vivid picture of Tudor society as it actually was.

Alexander McKee
How We Found the Mary Rose, 1982

The *Vasa* saved from the water

In 1961 the flagship of the Swedish fleet was raised to the surface after 333 years at the bottom of Stockholm's harbour.

Over the centuries the site of the disaster had been forgotten. It was to be over three hundred years before a thirty-eight-year-old engineer, Anders Franzén, embarked on the search for this ghost ship. In his opinion the *Vasa* had clearly survived because it lay in the relatively fresh waters of the Baltic – and especially in Stockholm's harbour – where the salinity was too low for shipworm, a great devourer of wood in the normally salty waters of the sea.

On 25 August 1956, after five years of systematically examining archives and the sea floor, Anders Franzén, raised an important piece of evidence – a piece of blackened oak – with the little core sampler he had invented. A few days later the diver Edvin Fälting went down to the bottom of the sea and groped around in the total darkness with

his hands: 'I cannot see anything because it is completely black down there, but I feel something big. The side of a ship. Here is a port-hole, and another one. There are two rows of them. This must be the *Vasa*.'

The first problem – both financial and technical – to be resolved, was to refloat the ship. King Gustav VI took an active interest in the project; the Swedish navy supplied ships and personnel; the specialist salvage company Neptun found a solution

by offering to carry out the unique operation for free; a public subscription was launched.

In two years the divers, using a pressurized water jet, dug six tunnels underneath the *Vasa*. Through these they passed heavy wires, which were attached at each end to pontoons filled with water. Once the wires had been fed through and secured, the pontoons were partly emptied of their liquid content and – with Archimedes' help – they rose. In this way the *Vasa* was lifted off the mud without breaking the hull.

The hull was moved to shallower waters but left submerged: the 1000 tonnes of oak of which it was made were swollen with water (1.5 kg of water to 1 kg of wood [3lbs to 2lbs]) and could not be brought into the air for fear that they might contract and be more or less destroyed. Divers worked for two years to seal every opening in the hull so as to make it watertight.

A specially built laboratory
Finally, on 24 April 1961, the *Vasa* was hauled to the surface, emptied of water and some of the mud that filled it, and on 4 May the ship finally floated after 333 years spent on the bed of the port at Stockholm. It was then towed into a dry dock. The archaeological, conservation and restoration work could now begin.

It was only when the *Vasa* had been refloated that the problem of conserving an 'object' with 900 cubic metres of wood full of water had to be faced for the first time. In 1961 a laboratory was specially built for the conservation of the old ship. The chosen method was to impregnate the wood slowly with polyethylene glycol, following the

The *Vasa* starting to emerge from the water in Stockholm harbour.

procedure devised a few years earlier by Rolf Moren and Bertil Centervall. For obvious reasons the *Vasa* could not be immersed in a vat full of water and polyethylene glycol, so the ship was sprayed for twenty-five minutes with twenty-minute intervals. The whole process continued for twenty-four hours a day…for seventeen years.

In all, 250 tonnes of polyethylene glycol were used in spraying the ship repeatedly, according to Sven Bengtsson, who worked in the conservation laboratory of the *Vasa* from 1961. The temporary museum built around the *Vasa* was thus full of a damp mist, the old hull was streaming and the clothes of a great many visitors were splashed.

Little by little the polyethylene glycol penetrated the wood and remained there when the drying process, which was started in 1979 and is still not complete, began to get rid of the water. In the final museum, which was opened in June 1990, the *Vasa* bathes in a carefully controlled atmosphere (a relative humidity of 60 per cent and a temperature of 18° to 20° C [about 68 to 70° F], all the time) and its lighting is limited to 50 lux. The last 580 tonnes of water that should be completely eliminated from the wood of the ship will thus evaporate without damage.

Apart from impregnating the mass of wood from the hull, the surface of the latter was later sprayed with polyethylene glycol and any excess was removed by powerful currents of air at 80°C.

When it floated, the hull of the *Vasa* still contained a metre [about three feet] of thick black mud in which the archaeologists – duly vaccinated against various illnesses – waded about for five months and fished out 14,000 objects of all kinds. From the site of the wreck the divers had brought up other things: in fact, the *Vasa* had been damaged during several unsuccessful attempts to refloat her in the 17th century. Over fifty cannons were raised in 1664 and 1665, which, given the more rudimentary techniques of the period, was a remarkable achievement.

When it was brought up, the hull of the *Vasa* was still intact. But there were 13,500 parts that needed to be put back together (five hundred carved figures and various sculptures) coming mainly from the aftercastle, the ship's head and the upper deck. After treatment in vats, again full of water and polyethylene glycol, all these pieces were restored to their original places with such success that the *Vasa* now incorporates only 5 per cent new pieces. They stand out from the original 95 per cent by their lighter colour and smoother surface (but they are lightly carved to preserve an overall harmony). Thus we have the only complete framework of a 17th-century ship.

Restored to life
The 12,000 other recovered objects were made of wood, metal, fabric, leather, glass, pottery, all of which – apart from the last two – required special treatment. Leather, for example, was conserved by freeze-drying. Wool only had to be put out to dry. The six linen or hemp sails that were retrieved, on the other hand, had become as fragile as wet newspaper: so they were unfolded under water, very slowly laid flat, impregnated with a mixture of alcohol and xylene, dried and fixed to a support to be hung in the storerooms of the museum.

Yvonne Rebeyrol
Le Monde, 1 January 1992

A copper nail helps to identify the wreck of the *Méduse*

The search for the Méduse, *a French navy frigate lost fifty kilometres (thirty miles) off the coast of Mauretania, was a mission to apply geophysical survey techniques to underwater archaeology. Once the magnetic anomaly was located, the task was to identify the wreck site positively, within the limits of a survey operation.*

As the site was not to be excavated, no isolated find on the site could be regarded as conclusive evidence. Apart from a nail. This copper nail, square in section, bearing the initials 'F. R.', alone warranted thorough research, with what turned out to be definitive results. It was in fact common to find in the pegging of warships of the period an arsenal mark showing it to be state property....

It seemed that the letters 'F. R.' stood for 'Forges de Rochefort', Rochefort having been, with Toulon, the only arsenal, under the Ancien Régime, where the navy had copper worked into bronze artillery. But while the *Méduse* had indeed been armed at Rochefort for its voyage to the African coast in 1816, she had been built at Paimboeuf in a private naval shipyard, at a period when naval shipwrights under contract to the state were in most cases left to obtain their own materials, such as copper. The investigation stopped short at these questions....

Research in the archives at the port of Rochefort rapidly led to the theory 'F. R.' = 'Forges de Rochefort' being abandoned: it turned out that the Rochefort arsenal had only tried out casting copper nails at a very late date, in 1816, the year that the *Méduse*

was wrecked. Moreover, the research department of the Musée de la Marine in Paris has recently discovered in the naval museum at Rochefort exactly the same kind of copper nail, bearing the full inscription 'Romilly', as the one found at the Banc d'Arguin. It was then that an archivist-palaeographer at the Ecole des Chartes, M. Brunter'ch, who was working on the classification of a collection that had recently been placed in the provincial archives of Loire-Atlantique in Nantes, found an order placed by the builders of the *Méduse*, Crucy father and son, for a lot of copper nails the same size as the one found at the Banc d'Arguin. The order was dated 1806, the construction of the *Méduse* having started in Paimboeuf in 1807, and it had been addressed to an establishment in the Eure district specializing in the manufacture of copper articles for the navy, the Forges de Romilly.... This discovery shed light on the development of the copper industry in France, the way in which it was organized, and the role of private industry from the beginning of the revolutionary period under the pressure of technological innovation and political events. The Forges de Romilly was founded in 1781 at a time when copper, used in sheathed hulls and then their pegging, was introduced on a massive scale in shipbuilding for the navy, for which it soon became one of the main suppliers.... One of the tasks of underwater archaeological projects concerned with historical wrecks is to refine the dating of specific artefacts.

Jean-Yves Blot
'*La Méduse*', *La Recherche*
February 1983

Today the concern is to protect and preserve our past

Now that we can reach the ocean depths with the technology available in the late 20th century, there is a great debate over what should be done with the underwater remains thus exposed. Should they be destroyed or sold? Or how can those material remains that constitute our roots, including human skeletons, be preserved and protected?

Neptune's notaries

In contrast to land archaeology, where there is a clear sense of a cultural heritage and of the role of those working in the field, underwater archaeology remains a legal minefield, subject of a continual debate over the respective roles of various groups, including the public and a small industry devoted to the commercial exploitation of archaeological sites.

Myths sometimes take root, as proved by a piece of legislation drawn up in 1993 at the behest of the then Lisbon Secretariat for Culture. The Portuguese episode set a striking precedent within a European cultural context; in order to excavate an underwater site, bank guarantees to the tune of 1.5 million dollars [£1 million] were required, in the form of concessions capable of being assigned to sub-concessionaires, as with oil fields and mines. The concessionaire was to be remunerated by a share of the archaeological finds under water.

This 'business' element in the Portuguese legislation of 1993 worried UNESCO and the regional government of the Azores, which was very much concerned in the proceedings because the Azores lay on the return route for colonial merchant vessels. The legal position taken by the Portuguese, clearly aimed at the sale of 'repetitive' objects – porcelain from the east, precious metal coins and similar cargo – sacrificed in the short term all research on sites without 'commercial' potential. The law adopted in Lisbon in 1993 assigned only a minor role to 'non-commercial' sites, for which special authorization had to be obtained.

The diver Edvin Fälting holding a human skull from the wreck of the *Vasa*.

The shipwreck of the *Santa Maria* in a 19th-century engraving.

The legislation was frozen in late 1995 by the newly created Ministry of Culture. The Portuguese episode has raised a question that would have been unthinkable on land: can these finds be sold?

The British archaeologist Margaret Rule has answered in the affirmative, on the condition that every artefact raised during an underwater excavation has already been studied and has received a 'pedigree' (sic).

Such a standpoint, taken by the director of the *Mary Rose* excavations, marks a turning point in a debate that has continued for years in Anglo-Saxon circles: in an editorial entitled 'Crisis in Nautical Archaeology' published in the scientific review *International Journal of Nautical Archaeology* in 1986, Valerie Fenwick, a representative of the British Nautical Archaeology Committee, expressed concern over collections taken from underwater sites being auctioned and criticized archaeologists under contract with the firms for supporting commercial ventures. Four years later the same scientific review noted that, between 1983 and 1986, 190,000 pieces of porcelain were sold at auction by Christie's after the Singapore salvage operator Michael Hatcher had raised two ancient cargoes in international waters. The position adopted by Margaret Rule and the recent Portuguese law suggests that such questions have ceased to be an issue for the Caribbean or for southeast Asia and have now entered European cultural territory.

Two recent experiences have provided an important, alternative answer to the whole question. The first, a venture by the North American company RMS Titanic Inc., has led to a collection of objects from the site of the *Titanic* being retrieved, with the help of the French IFREMER team and its submarine *Nautile*. Many people in Anglo-Saxon political and cultural circles strongly opposed any of the artefacts being raised at all and supported the idea of leaving the *Titanic*, which took 1523 people to their deaths when it sank in 1912, as an inviolable shrine.

Instead of 'selling' the artefacts raised from the *Titanic*, the New York firm undertook not to break up the collections but to repay its shareholders by organizing public exhibitions of the collections, such as the one held at the National Maritime Museum in Greenwich. In a poll of the 27,196 visitors to the exhibition, 72 per cent were of the opinion that further objects should be brought up from the site of the *Titanic* on future research trips.

The research carried out in the Philippines by World Wide First, a firm that specializes in excavating ancient wrecks and is headed by the French financier Franck Goddio, seems to work on the same principle. Artefacts from the wreck of the Spanish warship the *San Diego*, which sank off Manila in 1600, were recently put on show.

Such projects are at the opposite extreme to the everyday work of volunteers who have played a key role since the early days of this scientific discipline fifty years ago. Exploring the past was for a long time – under water or on land – a matter of passion, a driving force that could easily die out in the cold labyrinths of administration.

Recent French legislation on underwater archaeology, which places more constraints than ever before on the many amateurs involved in it, has led to a sudden drop in the number of reported sites found by divers in French waters. What will become of the social structure of a discipline that has always, all over the world, relied on the discoveries of outsiders (divers, fishermen, weekend sailors) and on the energy of divers, the driving spirits behind countless excavation sites?

Jean-Yves Blot
August 1995

The case of the *Alabama*: new legal factors

In 1872, seven years after the end of the Civil War, the United States government obtained at Geneva a payment from Britain of 15.5 million gold dollars in compensation for its support of the deadly activities of the Confederate cruiser Alabama, *which had finally been sunk during an engagement off Cherbourg in 1864. The recently located wreck has led lawyers to take a fresh interest in the* Alabama, *before making way for archaeologists.*

On 19 June 1864, after an hour's battle against the USS *Kearsarge*, the CSS *Alabama* sank seven miles [eleven km]

On the wreck of the *Alabama*.

off Cherbourg. Two hours earlier the French flagship the *Couronne* had escorted the *Alabama* outside territorial waters, then set at three miles [nearly five km], so that the battle took place in international waters.

However, when in 1962 France extended its territorial waters to twelve miles [nineteen km], the United States took note of the decision and made clear that they maintained their rights of ownership over the *Alabama* if the wreck were ever discovered.

In November 1984 the minesweeper *Circé* discovered a wreck that was identified as being, in all probability, that of the *Alabama*. The news was officially reported in the United States, at Charleston, in September 1987, at the same time as an excavation project was set up by a Franco-American team directed by Commandant Guérout.

The affair took a sharp polemical turn with the start of negotiations between the French Ministry of Foreign Affairs and the American State Department. A British team from Liverpool applied to bring the refloated wreck of the *Alabama* back to dock 4 at Birkenhead, where it had been built, and several American teams vied with each other to take the wreck back to the United States. With that aim two bills were submitted, one in the House of Representatives, the other in the Senate. The first, S. 2093, entitled 'Preservation of the CSS *Alabama* Act', was submitted on 23 February 1988 by Senator Howell Heflin of the state of Alabama.

The second, H. R. 1563, entitled 'CSS *Alabama* Preservation Act', was tabled on 22 March 1989 by Walter B. Jones, a Representative from the state of Georgia, in his name and in the name of several Representatives from the states of North Carolina and Georgia,

'to preserve the United States title and interest in the CSS *Alabama* and encourage its preservation'.

In 1988 Guérout had been authorized by the French Ministry of Culture to take soundings on the site.

On 3 October 1989 the two countries concerned reached agreement. Without actually settling the problem of who owned the wreck, this agreement created a scientific committee with Franco-American parity charged with examining requests to excavate the wreck of the *Alabama* and submitting an opinion to the French authorities responsible for authorizing excavation. The United States' ownership of the wreck was recognized shortly after by the French Ministries of Culture and Foreign Affairs.

What comes into play here is, on the one hand, the fact that the wreck lies within French territorial waters and, on the other, the principle recognized by all great maritime nations that the wrecks of warships, wherever they may be found, remain the property of the nation whose flag they displayed unless they had surrendered to the enemy. What posed a problem in the case of the *Alabama* was whether a warship of the Confederate States (the *Alabama* was not a privateer: it had all the attributes of a warship and its commander had an official letter of appointment) could be regarded as the property of the United States of America. It must be remembered that the states of the South had not been recognized by the North and were considered as rebels. However, though countries such as Great Britain and France had not officially recognized the Confederacy, they had recognized the state of war. This nicety allowed them to treat the warships from the two sides on an equal footing when they called into port. The attitude came close to official recognition, since fitting out a warship effectively gives it official status. The Ministry of Foreign Affairs took this into account, as well as the fact that the *Alabama* was clearly an important piece of American history.

Two years went by before this commission, made up of two representatives from each country, met for the first time and five years before the excavation team, which had never abandoned its annual investigations, first obtained authorization for a proper excavation in 1994.

Finally, on 23 March 1995, seven years after the first dives had taken place, Dr Ulane Bonnel, president of the CSS *Alabama* Association that supported the archaeological project, signed an 'agreement' with the United States government recognizing the association as operator and defining everyone's rights and duties.

This long procedure was the first time international parties had cooperated over the excavation of an underwater archaeological site. But there is no doubt that it will be difficult to have this legal precedent accepted by all the nations whose territorial waters contain the remains of warships. Indeed, while nations with a maritime tradition may accept the reciprocal principle of this law, the same is not true of most other countries, who consider that wrecks in their territorial waters are their property.

Max Guérout
25 August 1995

The *Titanic*

As a symbol of the modern age, the Titanic *stirs strong feelings.*

The *Titanic*, especially, has roused strong emotions over the question of 'to-touch' or 'not-to-touch'. A bill was even introduced into the United States Senate that would have prevented import into the United States of any of the artefacts being raised from the vessel. But this is not an archaeological matter. The *Titanic* is no more an archaeological site than is the *Andrea Doria*, yet there have been no outcries about disturbing the latter. It is said that the *Titanic* should not be disturbed because lives were lost during her sinking, but such reasoning would put both salvors and nautical archaeologists out of business around the world.....

The debate over historic preservation on land – are we saving too much? – Are we saving the right things? – must include historic preservation under water. It would seem wrong to allocate large sums for the preservation of one ship simply because she lies on the ocean floor, when an identical sister ship, rotting at her moorings, might legitimately and ethically be cut up and sold for scrap. Yet some preservationists seem still not to recognize this double standard.

With tens or even hundreds of thousands of wrecks in the Americas, the public may believe that this debate over what to save may be postponed, but such is not the case. Although only a fraction of existing wrecks warrant archaeological excavation, it is exactly that fraction – wrecks of historical importance, or those rich in artefacts – that attract treasure-hunters who are not motivated by the desire to recover and restore the past of the Americas.... All the known wrecks of the Age of Exploration were damaged by

A suitcase from the wreck of the *Titanic* lies on the sea floor, an eerie reminder of the passengers who died in the disaster.

modern looters before archaeologists reached them....

Society must decide, then, which wrecks should be protected from commercial exploitation, just as society protects certain structures on land while others of equal vintage are razed. In some cases this is easy. We would not allow an entrepreneur to dismantle either Mount Vernon or the Alamo for private gain. Why, then, should a diver be allowed to dismantle one of Columbus' or La Salle's ships to sell or own for personal benefit? Some historic wrecks should be preserved through excavation and conservation; others should be preserved under water for the pleasure of future generations of visiting divers.

Society must also decide the cost it will bear in order to learn about and preserve the past. In the near future, new knowledge will continue to come from relatively shallow or even underground wrecks. Will archaeology be able to take advantage of the new technologies to search and work deeper? Only the tiniest fraction of the millions spent on the H-bomb search would ever be available for seeking an archaeological site under similar conditions. The United States was willing to pay the necessary millions of dollars for the *Titanic* search primarily because it provided a test of equipment with potential military value. The cost of saturation diving on HMS *Edinburgh* was more than offset by the value of the gold recovered.

Archaeologists will not come by such vast sums in their search for knowledge. Should deep wrecks then be left to entrepreneurs who might pay for their recovery through sales of artefacts? Or should they be saved for the future, when new techniques could lower costs of working at great depth?

Education must play a role in the study of whichever wrecks do warrant archaeological study. Although often commendable, some…pioneering research…was conducted by divers with only a smattering of historical knowledge, or by archaeologists with scant familiarity with ship design….

Humans being fallible, mistakes will be made in the attempt to draw distinctions between wrecks of social or historic significance and those of more commercial value. 'Significance' is in the eye of the beholder. Yet the public has agreed that looters should not be allowed to bulldoze any native American mounds for pottery to sell. The public should come to see historic monuments under water simply as historic monuments.

At the same time the public, and especially the news media, must recognize the difference between those who excavate historic ships for knowledge and those who recover them solely for monetary gain. The press too quickly bestows the title 'underwater archaeologist' on any diver who raises artefacts from the deep. There is a long and honourable tradition of salvage at sea, but it must not be confused with archaeology.

George F. Bass and W. F. Searle
'Epilog' in George F. Bass (ed.)
*Ships and Shipwrecks of the Americas:
A History Based on Underwater
Archaeology*, 1988

The *Titanic*: a history of corrosion

The artefacts on the wreck, which is regularly visited by both scientists and industrialists, are steadily deteriorating in international waters. The Titanic *presents an enormous challenge to conservators who are entrusted with halting the complex processes of gradual destruction.*

In the complete darkness in the depths of the Atlantic, one might think that time had been virtually suspended, that no chemical or physical changes could take place and that the carcass of the *Titanic*, once over the shock of its enormous mass descending on the hard ocean floor, barely covered by a few centimetres of powdery sediment, would lie for all eternity in a silent environment where the only perceptible change is on a geological scale.

In fact, this is not the case, and the apparent beauty of the wreck shown on films taken by underwater cameras or the beauty of some of the artefacts that have been raised masks the reality of a pernicious ailment that is, little by little, devouring them. The slow corrosions to which we refer (chemical decay under the action of chlorides and sulphides, galvanic corrosions caused by the contact of different metals) inoculate the metals with chemicals that act as catalysts when the object is exposed to the air. The effect of one of the best known chemicals – anion chloride – on iron objects taken from the ocean has long been under study. In order to limit this cycle of destruction, it is essential to avoid exposing the porous material to oxygen in the air.

In order to conserve metal objects, it is essential to follow these rules:
– keep the object away from oxygen
– start the process of extracting noxious elements (chlorides) quickly.

As soon as artefacts are removed from the water, they are placed in a supply of fresh water, and we have asked that among other precautions, they should be exposed to the air as little as possible – just long enough for scientists to examine them and for photographers to record them.

Objects from the wreck of the *Titanic*: plates brought up in 1988, before (left) and after (right) restoration.

The conservation of artefacts raised from the *Titanic* is somewhat different, it is true, from the usual work of the EDF [Electricité de France] that is essentially aimed at the conservation of artefacts and objects of archaeological interest using electro-chemical techniques.

However, materials that had been altered in different ways after lying for a period of seventy-five years 4000 metres [13,120 feet] deep southeast of Newfoundland provided the EDF conservation specialists with a particularly interesting field of study. This unique project revealed that the theory of corrosion did not explain the real state of exhumed objects, particularly metals. It is now possible to understand how different types of corrosion occur and to treat it more effectively with low-potential electrolytic dechloridation, as specified by the EDF laboratories.

During these investigations, a series of observations and analyses were conducted on large pieces of copper alloy from the *Titanic*.... Our first objective was to examine the alloys, among the more characteristic objects; the second consisted in studying both the site in physio-chemical terms and the way in which the position of objects in the substratum affected them. This article records our observations and conclusions on this subject.

Various copper alloys raised from the *Titanic* – such as engine parts, heavy navigational instruments, decorative features, chandeliers, bench arm-rests, bathroom fittings, the deck bell – really have only one thing in common: their material, which consists principally of a copper/tin or copper/zinc alloy with a few variations in composition depending on the use to which they were put. They are either of standard or nautical quality, the latter generally differing from the former in the substitution for tin of zinc, which, as bronze goes, provides better resistance to corrosion. The fact that all these copper alloys are in such disparate states of conservation has confirmed the complexity of the different processes at work on the wreck.

Paul Mardikian and Noël Lacoudre
'Le *Titanic*, une histoire de corrosion'
Neptunia, 1990

Clandestine passengers: rats

As early as the Yuan dynasty in China (13–14th centuries), damage caused by rats on board ships was mentioned in financial accounts. In 1836 Charles Darwin noted the presence of rats in the remote archipelago in Cocos Keeling in the Indian Ocean. According to him, the rats had come from Mauritius Island and had landed with a shipwreck. Since then, archaeologists have found underwater remains, in Australia, Texas and elsewhere, of the early clandestine voyages of 'man's worst enemy'.

It is well documented that Spanish ships sailing to the New World in the 16th and 17th centuries unwittingly carried with them roof rats (also appropriately known as ships' rats); and the skeletal remains of these rodents have recently been discovered in the wreck of the Basque whaling galleon *San Juan*, which sank off Canada's Labrador coast in 1565…. Undoubtedly, Dutch, French and English ships sailing to North

Skeleton of a 30–35-year-old sailor caught under a gun-carriage on the *Vasa*.

America and the Caribbean during this period also carried *Rattus rattus* as unwelcome passengers. Conclusive proof of their presence on English ships has now come from the *Sea Venture*, which yielded one metatarsal bone from the hind foot of a roof rat….

According to Professor Jackson, Director of the Environmental Studies Center, Ohio State University, the rat is perhaps 'man's worst enemy'; and on board ships such as the *Sea Venture* such creatures potentially could have wrought great damage by scavenging among the stored provisions, contaminating the foodstuffs with their urine and faeces, and spoiling preserved meat through damage to the wooden storage casks….

In addition to spoiling foodstuffs, rats on the early transatlantic ships also must have carried various zoonoses (diseases that could be transmitted to humans) including leptospirosis, murine typhus, and perhaps most feared of all, bubonic plague. Fortunately, the sailors and passengers on board the *Sea Venture* apparently did not suffer any of these diseases.

In order to control rat infestation, a ship's cat was a necessity on the early voyages to the New World; and it is therefore no surprise to find that the *Sea Venture* carried such an animal; which alas perished when the vessel sank, as evidenced by the presence in the wreck of a felid fibula bone.

Philip L. Armitage
'Victuals and Vermin: Life on Board
the *Sea Venture* in 1609'
*Bulletin of the Institute of Maritime
History and Archaeology*
December 1987

The navigator and his skeleton

The notable absence in most wrecks is man – the shipwrecked person. This apparent paradox is due in part to the marine worms that devour organic matter. However, the archaeology of the shipwreck goes beyond the marine environment as a great number of the victims' bodies are carried to the shore, where the local people bury them, in one way or another, in the days or weeks following an accident. It is easy to forget that a site in water often has a corresponding one on land, containing the remains of the humans involved in the disaster.

This archaeology of death in water, which concentrates on analysing the human skeleton and the information it gives, is thus practised to a large extent on land. Brutal deaths, bodies torn to pieces by the wood of the hull or rocks on the shore, smashed skulls, entrails full of marine sediment – the archaeology of the shipwrecked person on land provides in minute detail a portrait of an individual, whether master or slave, sailor or prisoner, who gave life to the vessel on the water.

Jean-Yves Blot
September 1995

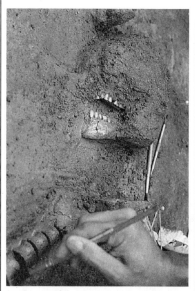

The smashed skeleton of a victim from the warship *San Pedro de Alcántara* which foundered on the coast of Peniche in Portugal in 1786 carrying Peruvian prisoners from the Indian rebellion of the leader José Gabriel Tùpac Amaru. The drowned people – unusually, 128 men and women of different races – are part of the archaeological research which started on land in 1985, and which was later followed by the study of the underwater site.

FURTHER READING

Arnold, J. Barto, and Robert Weddle,
   *The Nautical Archaeology of Padre Island:
   The Spanish Shipwrecks of 1554*, 1978

Ballard, Robert D., with Rick Archbold,
   The Discovery of the Titanic, 1987

Bascom, Willard, *Deep Water, Ancient Ships:
   The Treasure Vault of the Mediterranean*, 1976

Bass, George F., *Archaeology Under Water*, 1966

— (ed.), *A History of Seafaring Based on
   Underwater Archaeology*, 1972

— (ed.), *Ships and Shipwrecks of the Americas:
   A History Based on Underwater Archaeology*,
   1988

—, and F. H. van Doorninck, *Yassi Ada. Volume
   I. A Seventh-Century Byzantine Shipwreck*,
   1982

Benoît, Fernand, *Fouilles sous-marines: L'Epave
   du Grand Congloué à Marseille, Gallia*
   Supplement 14, 1961

Blot, Jean-Yves, *Archéologie sous-marine*, 1988

—, *Les Chasseurs de trésors du Gulf Stream*,
   1986

—, *La Méduse, chronique d'un naufrage ordinaire*,
   1982

Bruce-Mitford, Rupert L. S., *The Sutton Hoo
   Ship-Burial*, 3 vols., 1976, 1978, 1983

Cain, E., *Ghost Ships Hamilton and Scourge:
   Historical Treasures from the War of 1812*,
   1983

Casson, Lionel, *Ships and Seamanship in the
   Ancient World*, 1971

Evans, Angela Care, *The Sutton Hoo Ship Burial*,
   1986

Flemming, Nicholas C., *Cities in the Sea*, 1971

Franzén, Anders, *The Warship Vasa: Deep Diving
   and Marine Archaeology in Stockholm*, 1960

Frost, Honor, *Under the Mediterranean:
   Marine Antiquities*, 1963

Green, Jeremy N., *Australia's Oldest Wreck:
   The Historical Background and Archaeological
   Analysis of the Wreck of the English East India
   Company's Ship 'Trial', Lost off the Coast
   of Western Australia in 1622*, 1977

—, *Maritime Archaeology: A Technical Handbook*,
   1990

Greenhill, Basil, *Archaeology of the Boat*, 1976

Harding, Anthony Filmer, *The Lake Dwellings
   of Switzerland: Retrospect and Prospect*, 1980

Hasslöf, Olof, *Ships and Shipyards, Sailors and
   Fishermen: Introduction to Maritime Ethnology*,
   1972

Linder, Elisha, and Avner Raban, *Marine
   Archaeology*, 1975

Lockery, Andy, *Marine Archaeology and the
   Diver*, 1985

Long, Luc, 'Les Epaves du Grand Congloué.
   Etude du Journal de Fouilles de Fernand
   Benoît', *Archeonautica*, 1987

—, and Michel L'Hour and Eric Rieth, *Le
   Mauritius, la mémoire engloutie*, 1989

McKee, Alexander, *A History Under the Sea*,
   1968

—, *How We Found the Mary Rose*, 1982

Marx, Robert Frank, *Port Royal Rediscovered*,
   1973

—, *The Underwater Dig*, 1975

Muckelroy, Keith, *Archaeology Under Water:
   An Atlas of the World's Submerged Sites*,
   1980

—, *Discovering a Historic Wreck: A Handbook
   Offering some Advice on What to Do When
   You Find an Archaeological Site Under Water*,
   1981

—, *Maritime Archaeology*, 1978

Oleson, John Peter (ed.), *The Harbours of
   Caesarea Maritima: Results of the Caesarea
   Ancient Harbour Excavation Project 1980–5*,
   2 vols., 1989 and 1994

Pawson, Michael, and David Buissert, *Port
   Royal, Jamaica*, 1975

Pearson, Charles E. (ed.), *El Nuevo Constante:
   Investigation of an Eighteenth-century Spanish
   Shipwreck off the Louisiana Coast*, 1981

Pearson, Colin (ed.), *Conservation of Marine
   Archaeological Objects*, 1987

Petersen, Mendell, *History Under the Sea:
   A Handbook for Underwater Exploration*,
   1965

Rule, Margaret, *The Mary Rose: The Excavation
   and Raising of Henry VIII's Flagship*, 1982

Rule, Nick, 'Some Techniques for Cost-effective
   Three-dimensional Mapping of Underwater
   Sites', *Computer Applications and Quantitative
   Methods in Archaeology*, 1995

Taylor, Joan du Plat (ed.), *Marine Archaeology:
   Developments during Sixty Years in the
   Mediterranean*, 1965

Throckmorton, Peter, *Diving for Treasure*, 1977

—, (ed.), *History from the Sea: Shipwrecks and
   Archaeology*, 1987

Ucelli, Guido, *Le Navi di Nemi*, 1950

Villié, Pierre, *Calvi I*, 1993

LIST OF ILLUSTRATIONS

The following abbreviations have been used: *a* above; *b* below; *c* centre; *l* left; *r* right; BN Bibliothèque Nationale, Paris; INA Institute of Nautical Archaeology, University of Texas A & M, College Station; MM Musée de la Marine, Paris

COVER

Front Archaeologists raising amphorae from the wreck of a 7th-century Byzantine ship at Yassi Ada, Turkey. Photograph. INA
Spine A 17th-century gun. Watercolour by John Deane, 1836. Science Museum, London
Back Excavations at the port of Alexandria in June 1995. Photograph Stéphane Compoint

OPENING

1a A 16th-century Italian ship known as the *Lomellina*. Painting (detail) by Cristoforo Grasso. Civico Museo Navale, Genoa
1b Reconstruction of the *Lomellina*, a shipwreck found near Villefranche-sur-Mer in 1979 by Max Guérout's team. Painting by Noël Blotti
2 A diver using an air lift on the wreck of the *Lomellina*. Photograph Christian Pétron/GRAN
3 A diver marks the different parts of the *Lomellina*. Photograph Eric Rieth/GRAN
4–5 Two divers taking measurements of the *Lomellina*. Photograph Christian Pétron/GRAN
6 Two divers taking measurements of the *Lomellina*. Photograph Christian Pétron/Diaf
7 A diver taking photographs of the *Lomellina*. Photograph Christian Pétron/GRAN
8 A diver cutting a section of the *Lomellina* with a chain saw. Photograph Christian Pétron/Diaf
9 A diver raising a piece of the hull from the *Lomellina*. Photograph J.-C. Hurtaux/GRAN
11 Bronze heads found in the sea near Brindisi. Photograph

CHAPTER 1

12 Imaginary diving suit. Watercolour in Pedro de Ledesma, *Pesca de perlas y busqueda de galiones*, 1623. Museo Naval, Madrid
13 Glass bottles recovered from the *Mary Rose*. Watercolour by John Deane, 1836. Science Museum, London

14a A Roman stele depicting the salvage of a Greek statue from the sea in the 1st century BC. Marble bas-relief. Museo Archeologico, Ostia
14b Portrait of Leon Battista Alberti. Engraving in Guido Ucelli, *Le Navi di Nemi*, 1950. BN
14–5 Alexander the Great explores the sea floor. French manuscript 9342, 15th century. BN
15 Portrait of Francesco Demarchi. Engraving in Guido Ucelli, *Le Navi di Nemi*, 1950. BN
16 A breathing tube-helmet being used. Engraving in Diego Ufano, *Artillery*, 1614. BN
16–7 Cargo being raised from wrecks in the Tiber. Engraving in Cornelius Meyer, *L'Arte di rendere fiumi navigabili*, 1969. BN
17 East frieze from the Parthenon, Acropolis, Athens. Photograph. British Museum, London
18a The close diving helmet invented by Auguste Siebe in 1839. Photograph. MM
18b The diving platform built by Annesio Fusconi on Lake Nemi. Engraving in Guido Ucelli, *Le Navi de Nemi*, 1950. BN
18–9 Objects recovered from Lake Nemi. Photograph. Ibid.
19c Mosaic found in Lake Nemi. Photograph. Ibid.
19r Statue of 'Piombino Apollo'. Bronze, 5th century BC. Louvre, Paris
20a The Deanes investigating the wreck of the *Royal George* in diving suits. Watercolour by John Deane, 1836. Science Museum, London
20b Various salvaged objects. Watercolour by John Deane, 1836. Science Museum, London
20–1 Wrought-iron gun found on the *Mary Rose*. Watercolour by John Deane, 1836. Science Museum, London
21 The *Mary Rose*, the warship of Henry VIII. 16th-century miniature. By permission of the Master and Fellows of Magdalene College, Cambridge. © Mary Rose Trust, Portsmouth
22–3a Iron swords found near La Tène. Photograph in Paul Vouga, *La Tène*, 1923. BN
22–3b Neolithic lake dwellings. Watercolour by K. Jauslin, 1891. By permission of Birkhäuser Verlag AG, Basle. Musée d'Histoire, Berne
23 Diving in Lake Geneva on 26 August 1854. Drawing by Alphonse Morlot, 1859. Musée d'Histoire, Berne
24 Silver-plated bronze bust of the Roman Emperor Magnentius found in the Saône c. 1860–70. Photograph. Jules Chevrier collection. Musée Denon, Chalon-sur-Saône

CHAPTER 6

INDEX

TEXT CREDITS

Grateful acknowledgment is made for use of material from the following works: (pp. 164–5) Philip L. Armitage, 'Victuals and Vermin: Life on Board the *Sea Venture* in 1609', *Bulletin of the Institute of Maritime History and Archaeology*, December 1987; courtesy of the Bermuda Maritime Museum. (pp. 138–40) George F. Bass, 'Oldest Known Shipwreck Reveals Splendors of the Bronze Age', *National Geographic Magazine*, December 1987; by permission of George F. Bass. (p. 148) George F. Bass, 'Underwater Archaeology: Key to History's Warehouse', *National Geographic Magazine*, July 1963; by permission of the National Geographic Society, Washington, D.C. (pp. 160–2) George F. Bass and W. F. Searle, 'Epilog' in George F. Bass (ed.), *Ships and Shipwrecks of the Americas: A History Based on Underwater Archaeology*, 1988; by permission of George F. Bass. (pp. 132–3) Nicholas Flemming, 'Ice Ages and Human Occupation of the Continental Shelf', *Oceanus*, Spring 1985; by permission of *Oceanus* magazine, © Woods Hole Oceanographic Institution, Woods Hole, MA. (pp. 148–9) Anna Marguerite McCann and Joann Freed, 'Deep-water Archaeology: A Late-Roman Ship from Carthage and an Ancient Trade Route near Skerki Bank off Northwest Sicily', *Journal of Roman Archaeology* supplementary series no. 13, Ann Arbor, 1994; ISBN 1–887829–13–X; available from, and reprinted by permission of, *Journal of Roman Archaeology*, 1216 Bending Road, Ann Arbor, MI 48103, USA; fax (USA) 313 662 3240. (pp. 150–1) Alexander McKee, *How We Found the Mary Rose*, Souvenir Press Ltd, 1982; by permission of Souvenir Press Ltd, London. (p. 141) Colin Renfrew and Paul Bahn, *Archaeology: Theories, Methods and Practice*, Thames and Hudson, 1996; by permission of Lord Renfrew of Kaimsthorn and Dr Paul G. Bahn. (p. 147) Nick Rule, 'Some Techniques for Cost-effective Three-dimensional Mapping of Underwater Sites', *Computer Applications and Quantitative Methods in Archaeology*, BAR International Series 598, 1995; by permission of Nick Rule. (pp. 136–8)

Peter Throckmorton, 'Oldest Known Shipwreck Yields Bronze Age Cargo', *National Geographic Magazine*, May 1962; by permission of the National Geographic Society, Washington, D.C.

ACKNOWLEDGMENTS

The author and publisher wish particularly to thank Maria-Luisa Pinheiro-Blot, Commandant Max Guérout (GRAN), Luc Long (DRASM), Paul Mardikian (Archéolyse), André Lorin, and also Patrick Mouton, Azedine Beschaouch (UNESCO), Loïc Menanteau, Richard Clavaud, Nicholas Flemming, Jon Carpenter and Patrick Baker (Western Australian Maritime Museum), François Pignet (Editions Carré), Lars Einarsson (Kalmar Läns Museum), Eric Rieth and Madame Huyghes des Etages (Musée de la Marine, Paris), Nan Godet (Bermuda Maritime Museum), J. Barto Arnold III (Texas Antiquities Committee), Claude Huyghens and Marie-Jeanne Lambert (Musée d'Archéologie, Lons-le-Saulnier), Sjoerd de Meer (Maritime Museum, Rotterdam), Monsieur Nicolas (IFREMER), Louis Bonnamour (Musée Denon, Chalon-sur-Saône), Ignacio del Hierro and Cruz Apestegui (Madrid), Maria Jacobsen (INA, University of Texas A & M), Michel Egloff and Marc-Antoine Kaeser (Musée Cantonal d'Archéologie, Neuchâtel), Yvonne Rebeyrol, Vasamuseet, Palais du Roure in Avignon, Peabody Museum, Alexis Rosenfeld, Revue Maritime (Poidebard, Tyre), National Geographic Society, Dr Anatoly Sagalevitch, Robert Grenier and Daniel LaRoche (Parks Canada), Woods Hole Oceanographic Institution, Luis Falcao da Fonseca (Lisbon), Isabelle Bouvier (Public Library, Annecy), Jacques Ertaud, Hervé Miéville (Neuchâtel University), George Tulloch (RMS Titanic Inc., New York), Cynthia Dunning (Musée Schwab, Biel).

PHOTO CREDITS

Jean-Yves Blot
has first-hand experience of underwater archaeology,
having carried out excavations and surveys in three
oceans. He has published several books on his
investigations, including *La Méduse, chronique d'un
naufrage ordinaire* (1982), *Les Chasseurs de trésors du
Gulf Stream* (1986) and *Archéologie sous-marine* (1988).

For the San Pedro de Alcántara *excavation team*

© Gallimard 1995

English translation © Thames and Hudson Ltd,
London, 1996

Translated by Alexandra Campbell

British Library Cataloguing-in-Publication Data

A catalogue record for this book is available
from the British Library

ISBN 0–500–30068–2

Printed and bound in Italy
by Editoriale Libraria, Trieste